C   & Easy Knitting

Cute & Easy Knitting

Learn to knit with these 35 adorable projects

Fiona Goble

CICO BOOKS
LONDON NEW YORK

Published in 2013 by CICO Books
An imprint of Ryland Peters & Small
519 Broadway, 5th Floor, New York NY 10012
20–21 Jockey's Fields, London WC1R 4BW
www.rylandpeters.com

10 9 8 7 6 5 4 3 2 1

Editor: Marie Clayton
Designer: Julie Bennett
Artworks: Stephen Dew
Photographer: Caroline Arber
Stylist: Sophie Martell and Nel Haynes

A CIP catalog record for this book is available from the British Library.

ISBN: 978-1-78249-041-8

Printed in China
For digital editions visit www.cicobooks.com/apps.php

Contents

CHAPTER 1
Getting Started 26

CHAPTER 2
Getting Better 54

CHAPTER 3
Now You Are Really Good 98

Introduction

While I love traditional knitted items, for this collection I wanted to create something a bit different. I wanted the designs to be pretty, quirky—and to have a slightly vintage feel. In other words, I wanted to produce a range of knitted items that I'd like to have in my own home—or, in some cases, round my own neck or on my own hands! The collection includes patterns for newbie knitters as well as seasoned pros—and just about every stage in between.

I've divided the collection into three sections. The patterns in the first part are suitable for those who have just started to knit but still want to produce something lovely—either for themselves or as a gift.

In the second part the projects are aimed at knitters who have mastered the basics; they're up for something of a challenge but don't want anything too fancy or intricate. If you think this might be you but you haven't picked up your needles for a while, have a look through the Knitting Know-how section that begins on page 8. I think knitting is a bit like riding a bike—once you've learned how to do it, it's easy to get going again even after a bit of a break.

In the final part of the book, I've included projects for slightly more experienced knitters. But don't worry too much—this isn't a book for people who want to embark on projects that take several months of solid knitting, or those who want to spend their entire pay packet on knitting yarns.

And while on the subject of yarns, all the projects in the book are knitted in standard yarns. If you can't find the one specified or simply want to knit the item in something different, then choose a similar yarn of the same thickness. Remember to knit your gauge (tension) square first, though, to make sure that you are happy with the look and that your finished creation will be the right size.

For me, the most satisfying thing about knitting is how you can create such gorgeous items from something so simple—just a pair of knitting needles and a ball of yarn. All right, I admit that you usually also need a needle to sew your project together and a few adornments, but I'm sure you know what I mean.

I have loved working out the patterns in this book and I hope you will have fun recreating the items, perhaps in your own colors or with your own unique twist. I would love to hear how you get on—so please feel free to contact me via my blog at fionagoble.wordpress.com.

Tools & materials

The knitting needles, yarn, and other items that you need are listed at the beginning of each of the pattern instructions.

Knitting needles

Standard knitting needles can be made of metal, bamboo, or plastic and which type you choose is a matter of personal preference. The different sizes are based on the needle diameter but they also come in different lengths. Choose shorter needles for smaller projects because you will find them easier to work with.

• A couple of projects in this book use a circular knitting needle, which has a point at each end and a flexible section in the middle, usually made of plastic. Because they are much longer than standard needles you can use them to knit extra-wide projects such as the Stripy Throw (see page 118) and Lampshade (see page 106). Circular needles also enable you to knit a tube although we do not use them in this way in the projects in this book.

Pins

Pins can be used to hold pieces of knitting together before you sew. You can get special pins for knitting but any long pins with large heads will work fine.

Cable needle

These are short needles with a point on each end, used to make a cable pattern in your knitting. Sometimes they have a dip in the middle to help make sure your stitches stay in place on the needle.

Scissors

A small pair of sharp scissors is a vital tool for all knitters. They are used for snipping the yarn once your work is finished, and for trimming yarn tails after you have woven them in.

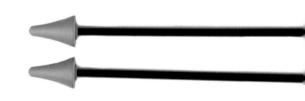

Point protectors

You can pop these over the point of your needles when you are taking a break from your knitting. They will stop the needles poking through your knitting bag or basket and keep your stitches on the needle.

Tape measure or ruler

A tape measure or ruler is essential for checking your gauge (tension) square and measuring your work.

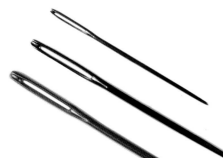

Yarn sewing and other needles

Large-eye yarn needles are used to sew your projects together. They are usually slightly blunt so that you do not split the yarn as you sew. Always choose the smallest size possible for the yarn used because this will make your work easier.

• For some projects you will also need an embroidery needle, which has a sharper point than a yarn sewing needle. Remember to select a needle with an eye large enough to thread the yarn.

• A standard sewing needle is used for sewing on buttons, snap fasteners, and other items.

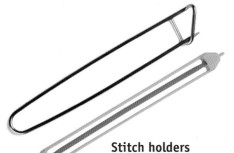

Stitch holders

These are useful to hold a group of stitches while you work on another part of your knitting.

Safety pins

Ordinary small safety pins are useful to mark particular stitches or rows that you will need to come back to later on. For some projects, you will also need a safety pin to thread trimmings or lengths of elastic through your work.

Water-soluble pen

These look like ordinary felt pens but the ink disappears when sprayed or dabbed with water. They are useful for marking particular points in your knitting where you want to embroider some finishing touches.

Pompom maker

These useful gadgets make creating pompoms quick and easy. However if you do not have one, you can always use two circles of cardboard with a hole cut in the center (see page 25).

Buttons

Some of the projects require buttons or other small embellishments. If you haven't already got one, it's a good idea to start a button collection so you have a few choices for your project.

Crochet hook

The projects in this book do not involve crochet as such, but some of them have a crochet edging (see page 25) or simple cord made of a length of crochet chain (see page 24). Crochet hooks are normally made of metal or plastic—the material you choose is up to you.

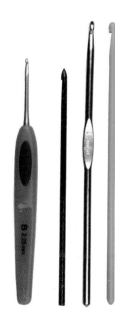

Fiberfill toy filling

You will need some fiberfill toy filling for some of the projects. It is specially made for stuffing handicrafts and soft toys, and is available from most haberdashery and craft stores. Check that the one you use conforms to all safety regulations.

Row counter

Some people find it helpful to have a row counter on one needle so they can keep track of where they are in their knitting pattern. Alternatively, you could simply make a note with a pencil and a piece of paper!

Yarn

The specific yarn required for each project is given in the instructions. You can substitute other yarns for those specified, but always make sure that the yarn you use is the same thickness, is made of a similar mix of fibers, and knits up to the recommended gauge (tension).

Substituting yarn

Balls of two different brands of the same type of yarn won't necessarily contain the same quantity of yarn— even if the balls weigh the same, it's the yardage (meterage) that's important. If the substitute yarn has a different yardage (meterage) per ball to the pattern yarn, then you need to do a sum to work out how many balls to buy.

1 Multiply the yardage (meterage) in one ball of pattern yarn by the number of balls needed to find out the total yardage (meterage) of yarn required.

2 Then divide the total yardage (meterage) by the yardage (meterage) in one ball of the substitute yarn to find out how many balls of that yarn you need to buy.

Example:
The pattern yarn has 109 yd (100 m) of yarn in each ball and you need 13 balls.
109 (100) x 13 = 1417 yd (1300 m) of yarn needed in total.

The substitute yarn has 123 yd (112 m) of yarn in each ball.
1417 ÷ 123 = 11.52 (1300 ÷ 112 = 11.6) So you only need to buy 12 balls of the substitute yarn.

Before buying all the substitute yarn, buy just one ball and knit a gauge (tension) swatch to be absolutely certain that you can get the right gauge (tension) with that yarn.

Working a gauge (tension) swatch

The gauge (tension) is given as the number of stitches and rows you need to work to produce a 4-in. (10-cm) square of knitting.

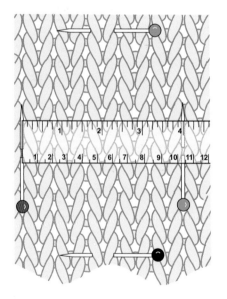

1 Using the recommended yarn and needles, cast on 8 stitches more than the gauge (tension) instruction asks for—so if you need to have 10 stitches to 4 in. (10 cm), cast on 18 stitches. Working in pattern as instructed, work eight rows more than is needed. Bind (cast) off loosely.

2 Lay the swatch flat without stretching it (the gauge/tension is given before washing or felting). Lay a ruler across the stitches as shown, with the 2 in. (5 cm) mark centered on the knitting, then put a pin in the knitting at the start of the ruler and at the 4 in. (10 cm) mark: the pins should be well away from the edges of the swatch. Count the number of stitches between the pins. Repeat the process across the rows to count the number of rows to 4 in. (10 cm).

If the number of stitches and rows you've counted is the same as the number asked for in the instructions, you have the correct gauge (tension). If you do not have the same number then you will need to change your gauge (tension).

To change gauge (tension) you need to change the size of your knitting needles. A good rule of thumb to follow is that one difference in needle size will create a difference of one stitch in the gauge (tension). You will need to use larger needles to achieve fewer stitches and smaller ones to achieve more stitches.

Abbreviations

These are the knitting abbreviations that you will need to know to follow the instructions in this book.

alt	alternate
beg	beginning
C4F	four-stitch front cable (see page 18)
C6B	six-stitch back cable (see page 19)
cont	continue
inc1	increase one stitch by knitting into the front then the back of the next stitch
K	knit
k2tog	knit the next 2 stitches together
kwise	insert right needle into the stitch as if to knit it
LH	left hand
M1	make one stitch by picking up the horizontal loop before the next stitch and knitting into the back of it.
P	purl
p2tog	purl the next 2 stitches together
patt	pattern
psso	pass slipped stitch over (the stitch just worked)
pwise	by purling the stitch or stitches
rep	repeat
rem	remaining
RH	right hand
RS	right side
s1	slip one (slip a stitch onto the right-hand needle without knitting it)
ssk	slip, slip, knit (slip 2 stitches one at a time then knit the slipped stitches together)
st(s)	stitch(es)
st st	stockinette (stocking) stitch
tbl	through back loop (work through the back loop of the stitch only)
WS	wrong side
yb	yarn back (see page 21)
yfwd	yarn forward (see page 21)
yo	yarn over (see page 21)
yo twice	yarn over twice (see page 21)
yrn	yarn round needle (see page 21)
cm	centimeter
g	gram
in.	inch
mm	millimeter
m	meter(s)
oz	ounce
yd	yard

[] Square brackets are used around instructions that you need to perform more than once. For example: [k2tog] 3 times means that you need to knit two stitches together three times.

() When you have worked a row to increase or decrease the number of stitches on your needle, the number of stitches you should have after completing the row is given in round brackets at the end. For example: (6 sts) means that you should have six stitches on your needle.

Techniques

If you're brand new to knitting or just want to refresh your skills, it's a good idea to grab your needles and a ball of yarn and practice a few basic techniques and stitches before you launch into your first project. These pages contain all the information you need to get going and are a resource to come back to when you come across a new technique.

Holding needles

If you are a knitting novice, you will need to discover which is the most comfortable way for you to hold your needles. This applies when using either a pair of knitting needles or a circular needle.

Like a pen
Now try changing the right hand so you are holding the needle as you would hold a pen, with your thumb and forefinger lightly gripping the needle close to its pointed tip and the shaft resting in the crook of your thumb. As you knit, you will not need to let go of the needle but simply slide your right hand forward to manipulate the yarn.

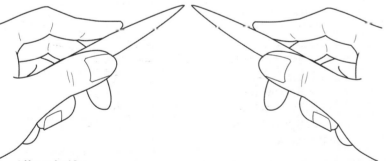

Like a knife
Pick up the needles, one in each hand, as if you were holding a knife and fork—that is to say, with your hands lightly over the top of each needle. As you knit, you will tuck the blunt end of the right-hand needle under your arm, let go with your hand and use your hand to manipulate the yarn, returning your hand to the needle to move the stitches along.

Holding yarn

As you knit, you will be working stitches off the left needle and on to the right needle, and the yarn you are working with needs to be tensioned and manipulated to produce an even fabric. To hold and tension the yarn you can use either your right or left hand. Try both methods to discover which works best for you.

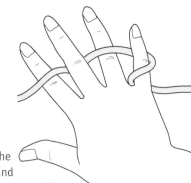

Yarn in right hand
With the ball of yarn on the right, catch the yarn around your little finger then lace it over the third finger, under the middle finger, and over the first finger of your right hand.

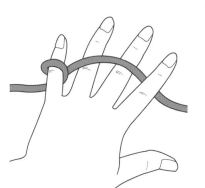

Yarn in left hand
With the ball of yarn on your left, catch the yarn around your little finger then take it over the third and middle fingers. Most left-handed knitters will also find that, even if they reverse the direction of knitting (working stitches off the right needle onto the left needle), using the left hand to manipulate the yarn will be easier to manage.

Making a slip knot

You will need to make a slip knot to form your first cast-on stitch.

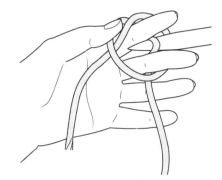

1 With the ball of yarn on your right, lay the end of the yarn on the palm of your left hand and hold it in place with your left thumb. With your right hand, take the yarn round your top two fingers to form a loop. Take the knitting needle through the back of the loop from right to left and use it to pick up the strand nearest to the yarn ball, as shown in the diagram. Pull the strand through to form a loop at the front.

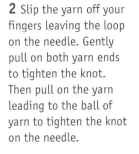

2 Slip the yarn off your fingers leaving the loop on the needle. Gently pull on both yarn ends to tighten the knot. Then pull on the yarn leading to the ball of yarn to tighten the knot on the needle.

Casting On (cable method)

There are a few methods of casting on but the one used for the projects in this book is the cable method, which uses two needles.

1 Make a slip knot as outlined on page 13. Put the needle with the slip knot into your left hand. Insert the point of your other needle into the front of the slip knot and under the left needle. Wind the yarn from the ball of yarn around the tip of the right needle.

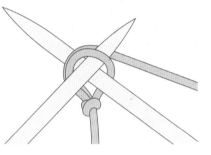

2 Using the tip of your needle, draw the yarn through the slip knot to form a loop. This loop is your new stitch. Slip the loop from the right needle onto the left needle.

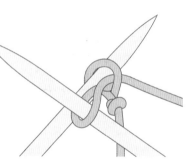

3 To make the next stitch, insert the tip of your right needle between the two stitches. Wind the yarn over the right needle, from left to right, then draw the yarn through to form a loop. Transfer this loop to your left needle. Repeat until you have cast on the right number of stitches for your project.

Casting on (thumb method)

This technique, sometimes called the thumb method, is usually considered to be the easiest and most versatile way of casting on.

1 Leave a long end of about ¾ in. (2 cm) per stitch to be cast on and then make a slip knot; the slip knot will be the first stitch. Holding the needle and the yarn from the ball in your right hand, use the free end of yarn to make a loop around your left thumb while at the same time keeping the yarn taut between the third and fourth fingers of your left hand. Insert the needle tip into the loop.

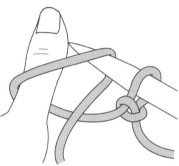

2 Bring the yarn from the ball up between your thumb and the needle then take it around the needle, as shown right.

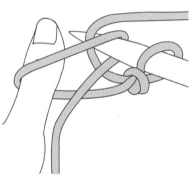

3 Draw the yarn through to make a stitch on the needle, then release the loop from the left thumb and gently pull on the yarn end to tighten the stitch on the needle.

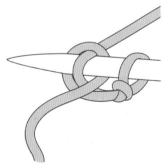

Basic Stitches

Most people in the English-speaking world knit using a method called English (or American) knitting. However, in parts of Europe, people prefer a method known as Continental knitting. If you are new to knitting, try both techniques to see which works better for you.

Making a knit stitch

1 Hold the needle with the cast-on stitches in your left hand, and then insert the point of the right needle into the front of the first stitch from left to right. Wind the yarn around the point of the right needle, from left to right.

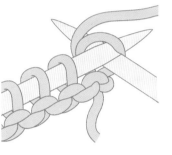

2 With the tip of your right needle, pull the yarn through the stitch to form a loop. This loop is your new stitch.

3 Slip the original stitch off the left needle by gently pulling your right needle to the right. Repeat these steps till you have knitted all the stitches on your left needle. To work the next row, transfer the needle with all the stitches into your left hand.

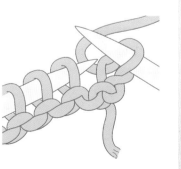

Continental style
Making a knit stitch

1 Hold the needle with the stitches to be knitted in your left hand, and then insert the tip of the right needle into the front of the first stitch from left to right. Holding the yarn fairly taut with your left hand at the back of your work, use the tip of your right needle to pick up a loop of yarn.

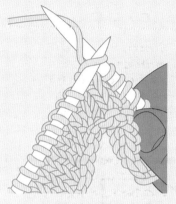

2 With the tip of your right needle, bring the yarn through the original stitch to form a loop. This loop is your new stitch.

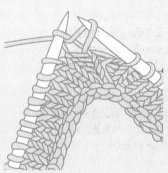

3 Slip the original stitch off the left needle by gently pulling your right needle to the right. Repeat these steps till you have knitted all the stitches on your left needle. To work the next row, transfer the needle with all the stitches into your left hand.

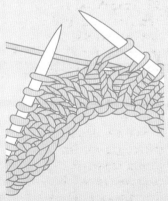

Making a purl stitch

1 Hold the needle with the stitches in your left hand, and then insert the point of the right needle into the front of the first stitch from right to left. Wind the yarn around the point of the right needle, from right to left.

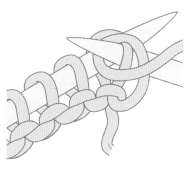

2 With the tip of the right needle, pull the yarn through the stitch to form a loop. This loop is your new stitch.

3 Slip the original stitch off the left needle by gently pulling your right needle to the right. Repeat these steps till you have purled all the stitches on your left needle. To work the next row, transfer the needle with all the stitches into your left hand.

Continental style
Making a purl stitch

1 Hold the needle with the stitches to be knitted in your left hand, and then insert the tip of the right needle into the front of the first stitch from right to left. Holding the yarn fairly taut at the back of your work, use the tip of your right needle to pick up a loop of yarn.

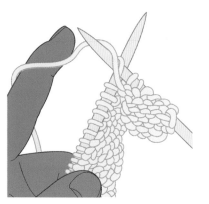

2 With the tip of your right needle, bring the yarn through the original stitch to form a loop.

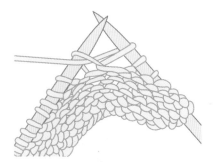

3 Slip the original stitch off the left needle by gently pulling your right needle to the right. Repeat these steps till you have purled all the stitches on your left needle. To work the next row, transfer the needle with all the stitches into your left hand.

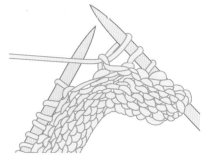

Binding (casting) off

In most cases, you will bind (cast) off knitwise, which means you will knit the stitches before you bind (cast) them off.

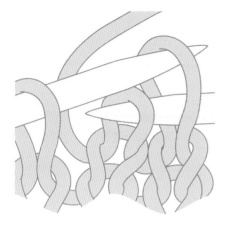

1 First knit two stitches in the normal way. With the point of your left needle, pick up the first stitch you have just knitted and lift it over the second stitch. Knit another stitch so that there are two stitches on your needle again. Repeat the process of lifting the first stitch over the second stitch. Continue this process until there is just one stitch remaining on the right needle.

2 Break the yarn, leaving a tail of yarn long enough to stitch your work together. Pull the tail all the way through the last stitch. Slip the stitch off the needle and pull it fairly tightly to make sure it is secure.

In a few of the projects in this book, you will need to bind (cast) off purlwise. This is exactly like ordinary binding (casting) off except that you purl the stitches rather than knit them.

Stockinette (stocking) stitch

This stitch makes a fabric that is different on each side; the knit side is flat and the purl side is textured.

To make this stitch, you work alternate rows of knit and purl stitches. The front of the fabric is the side when you work the knit rows.

Garter stitch

This stitch forms a ridged fabric that is the same on both sides.

To make this stitch, you simply knit every row.

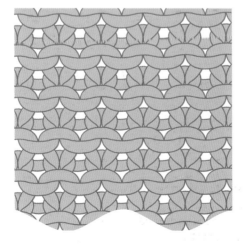

Cables

Create texture and pattern with cables by swapping the order in which you knit stitches. To create the cable you put a number of stitches on a cable needle and hold them in front (front cable) or behind (back cable) the work and then go back to them. Using a bent cable needle (see page 8) will make it even easier to hold the group of stitches being moved. The number given in the instruction refers to the total number of stitches over which the cable is being worked—so for C4F (as shown below) you only put two stitches on the cable needle.

Working a four-stitch front cable (C4F)

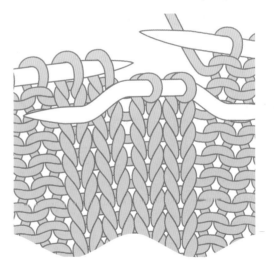

1 Work to the position of the cable. Slip the next two stitches on the left-hand needle onto the cable needle, keeping the cable needle in front of the work. Leave the two stitches on the cable needle in the middle so they don't slip off.

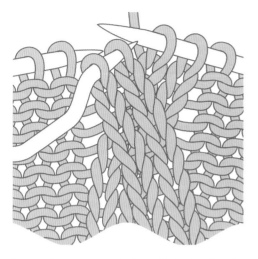

2 Knit the next two stitches off the left-hand needle in the usual way, then knit the two stitches off the cable needle and continue working from your pattern.

• Cable six forward (C6F)
As above, but hold three stitches at the front on the cable needle.

Working a six-stitch back cable (C6B)

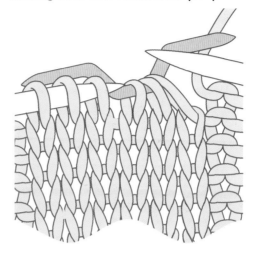

1 Work to the position of the cable. Slip the next three stitches on the left-hand needle onto the cable needle, keeping the cable needle at the back of the work. Leave the three stitches on the cable needle in the middle so they don't slip off.

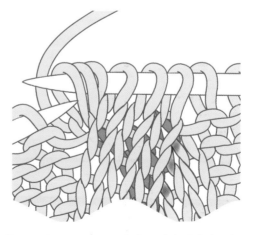

2 Knit the next three stitches of the left-hand needle in the usual way, then knit the three stitches off the cable needle and continue working from your pattern.

Shaping

You can shape your knitting pieces by increasing or decreasing the number of stitches on your needle. Each method results in a slightly different look.

Increasing

There are three main methods of increasing.

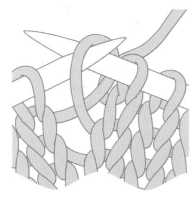

M1

Pick up the horizontal strand between two stitches on your left-hand needle. Knit into the back of the loop and transfer the stitch to the right-hand needle in the normal way. (It is important to knit into the back of the loop so that the yarn is twisted and does not form a hole in your work.)

inc1

Start knitting your stitch in the normal way but instead of slipping the "old" stitch off the needle, knit into the back of it and then slip the "old" stitch off the needle in the normal way.

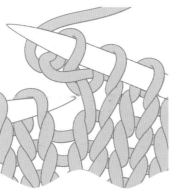

inc1 pwise

In a few of the patterns, you will also need to increase a stitch in this way on a purl row. This is done in the same way as increasing a stitch knitwise, except that you purl the stitches instead of knitting them.

Decreasing

There are several different ways of decreasing.

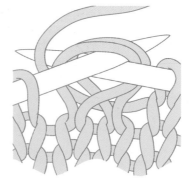

k2tog

This is the simplest way of decreasing. Simply insert your needle through two stitches instead of the normal one when you begin your stitch and then knit them in the normal way.

p2tog

Simply insert your needle through two stitches instead of one when you begin your stitch and then purl them in the normal way.

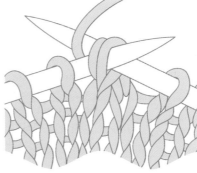

ssk

This is another way of decreasing. Slip one stitch and then the next stitch onto your right-hand needle, without knitting them. Then insert the left-hand needle from left to right through the front loops of both the slipped stitches and knit them as normal.

s1, k2tog, psso

This is a way of decreasing two stitches at a time. Slip the first stitch from the left to the right needle without knitting it. Knit the next two stitches together as described above. Then lift the slipped stitch over the stitch in front.

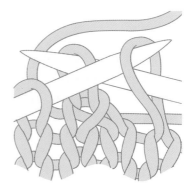

Slipping a stitch

Sometimes you will need to transfer a stitch from the right needle to the left needle, without knitting it. This is known as slipping a stitch and the instruction is written as S1.

Yarn overs

This is the general name given to the technique of making extra stitches and deliberate holes in your work by wrapping your yarn round your knitting needle to make loops. On the row following your yarn overs, treat the loops you have made in the same way as any other stitch.

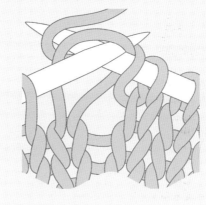

Yarn over (yo)

This is a way of creating an extra knit stitch between two existing stitches. Bring the yarn from the back to the front of your work, between your two needles. Knit the next stitch (or stitches) in the normal way, taking your yarn over the top of your right-hand needle as you do so to create the additional stitch.

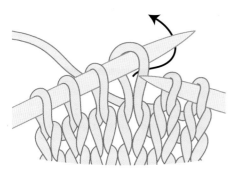

To slip a stitch, you simply insert your right-hand needle into the stitch in the normal way as if you were knitting it. Then instead of knitting the stitch, simply pull your right-hand needle further to the right so that the stitch "falls" off the left-hand needle and is transferred to the right-hand needle.

Yarn over twice (yo twice)

This is a way of creating two extra knit stitches between two existing stitches. Bring your yarn forward, as explained in the instruction above. Then take the yarn over the top of your right-hand needle and under it, so it is at the front of your work again. Knit the next stitch (or stitches) in the normal way, taking your yarn over the top of your right-hand needle as you do so to create your second additional stitch.

Yarn round needle (yrn)

This is a way of creating an extra purl stitch between two existing stitches. Bring the yarn from the front to the back of your work, between your two needles. Purl the next stitch (or stitches) in the normal way, taking your yarn over the top of your right-hand needle as you do so to create the additional stitch.

Yarn forward (yfwd)

This term is used when the yarn is at the back of the work (after a knit stitch has been made) but has to be put at the front before the next action is performed. Take the yarn from back to front between the two needles.

Yarn back (yb)

This term is used when the yarn is at the front of the work (after a purl stitch has been made) but has to be put to the back before the next action is performed. Take the yarn from front to back between the two needles.

Picking up stitches

For some projects, you will need to pick up stitches along either a horizontal edge (usually the cast-on edge of your knitting) or a vertical edge (the edges of your rows of knitting).

Along a vertical edge

This instruction is written as "pick up and k" as it involves picking up stitches and knitting them as you go along.

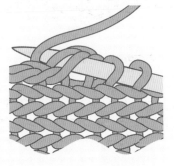

• With the right side of your knitting facing you, insert your needle from the front to back between the first and second stitches of the first row. Wind you yarn around the needle and pull through a loop to form the new stitch. Normally you have more gaps between rows than stitches you need to pick up and knit. To make sure your work is even, you will have to miss a gap every few rows.

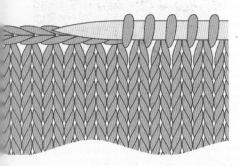

Along a horizontal edge

This is worked in the same way as picking up stitches along a vertical edge except that you will work through the cast-on stitches rather than the gaps between rows. You will normally have the same number of stitches to pick up and knit as there are existing stitches.

Sewing in ends

The easiest way to finish yarn ends is to run a few small stitches forwards then backwards through your work, ideally in a seam. It is a good idea to use your embroidery needle to do this and take the tail between the strands that make up your yarn, as this will help make sure the tail stays in place.

Knitting in different colors

If you are knitting in stripes, you can simply join your second color at one end. If the stripes are narrow, you do not need to break and rejoin your yarn between stripes.

Weaving

If you are knitting more than a few stitches in a different color, but only for a few rows, you can weave the yarns into the back of your stitches as you work.

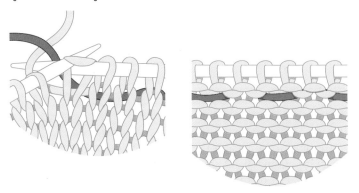

• On a knit row, insert your right-hand needle into the next stitch and lay the yarn you want to weave in over the needle. Knit the stitch, taking it under the yarn you are weaving in, making sure to pull through only the main yarn. Repeat this every few stitches until you need to use the second yarn again.
• On a purl row, use the same method to work in the yarn.

Stranding

If you are knitting just a few stitches in a different color, you can simply leave the color you are not using on the wrong side of your work and pick it up again when you need to.

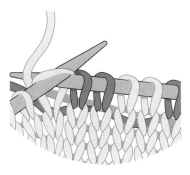

Color change (intarsia)

If you are knitting blocks of different colors within your project, you will need to use a technique called intarsia. This involves using separate balls of yarn for each area and twisting the yarns together where they join to avoid creating a gap.

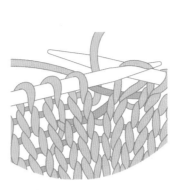

On the right side

When you want to change colors and the color change is vertical or sloping out to the right, take the first color over the second color. Then pick up the second color, so the strands of yarn cross each other.

On the wrong side

This is worked in almost the same way as on the right side. When you want to change colors and the color change is vertical or sloping out to the left, take the first color over the second color. Then pick up the second color, so the strands of yarn cross each other.

Finishing

Mattress stitch

There are two versions of this stitch – one used to join two vertical edges and the other used to join two horizontal edges.

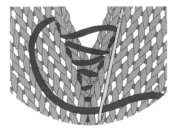 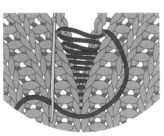

Vertical edges

Place the two edges side by side with the right side facing you. Take your needle under the running thread between the first two stitches of one side then under the corresponding running thread of the other side. Pull your yarn up fairly firmly every few stitches.

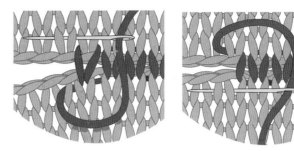

Horizontal edges

Place the two edges side by side with the right side facing you. Take your needle under the two "legs" of the last row of stitches on the first piece of knitting. Then take your needle under the two "legs" of the corresponding stitch on the second piece of knitting. Pull your yarn up fairly firmly every few stitches.

Flat seam

Unlike mattress stitch, this stitch creates a join that is completely flat.

• Lay the two edges to be joined side by side with the right side facing you. Pick up the very outermost strand of knitting from one side and then the other, working your way along the seam and pulling your yarn up firmly every few stitches.

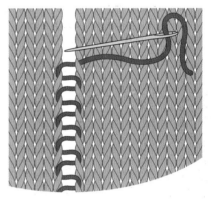

Oversewing

This stitch is used to seam small pieces of work. It is normally worked with the right sides of your work together.

• Take the yarn from the back of your work, over the edge of the seam and out through the back again a short distance further on.

Embroidery techniques

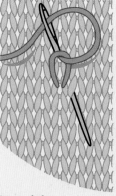

Chain stitch

Bring your yarn out at the starting point on the front of your work. Take your needle back into your knitting just next to your starting point, leaving a loop of yarn. Bring your needle out of your work again, a stitch length further on and catch in the loop. Pull your thread up firmly, but not so tight that it pulls your knitting. Continue in this way till the line, coil, or circle is complete.

Lazy daisy

Bring the needle and yarn up through the knitted fabric where you want the base of the petal to be, then take it back down through the fabric in the same place, leaving a loop of yarn on the front. Bring the tip of the needle up through the fabric, through the loop of yarn and back down on the other side of the loop to secure it in place. Repeat for each petal.

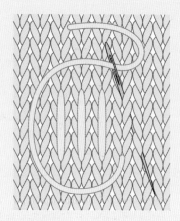

Straight stitch

To make this stitch, simply take your yarn out at your starting point and back down into your work where you want the stitch to end.

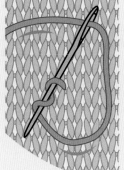
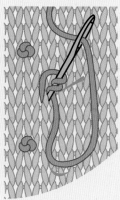

French knots

Bring your yarn out at your starting point, where you want the French knot to sit. Wind the yarn around the needle twice, then take it back into your work, just to the side of your starting point. Then take your needle out at the point for the next French knot or, if you are working the last or a single knot, to the back of your work. Continue pulling your needle through your work and slide the knot off the needle and onto your knitting.

Crochet techniques

While the projects in this book are all knitted rather than crocheted, for some projects you will need to know how to work a crochet chain or how to work a crochet edging.

Make a crochet chain

1 Make a slip knot on the crochet hook in the same way as if you were starting to cast on some knitting. Holding the slip stitch on the hook, wind the yarn round the hook from the back to the front, then catch the yarn in the crochet-hook tip.

2 Pull the yarn through the slip stitch on your crochet hook to make the second link in the chain.

3 Continue in this way till the chain is the length that you need.

Work a crochet edging

A crochet edging can be worked along a horizontal edge or a vertical edge, but the basic technique is the same.

1 Insert your crochet hook in the first space between stitches. Wind the yarn round the hook and pull a loop of yarn through.

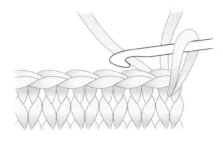

2 Wind the yarn round your hook again and then pull the loop through to make a single chain.

3 Insert your hook through the next stitch, wind the yarn round the hook, and pull through a second loop of yarn.

4 Wind the yarn round your hook and pull a loop of yarn through both loops on the hook. Repeat steps 3 and 4, inserting the hook into the spaces between stitches in an even pattern.

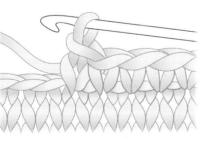

• For crochet edging along a vertical edge, insert your hook into the spaces between the edges of your rows rather than the spaces between stitches.

Pompoms

1 You can either use a pompom maker or make your own. Draw around something with a diameter of about 4 in. (10 cm) onto two pieces of stiff cardstock or cardboard (a cereal carton works well). Draw a smaller circle inside (draw around a large button or a cotton reel). Cut out the larger circle then cut out the inner circle.

2 Keep the 2 circles held together and wrap the yarn through the ring, wrapping it closely together. Don't wrap it too tightly or it will be difficult to slide in the scissors to cut.

3 When it is closely packed with yarn all the way around, carefully cut through the wraps of yarn around the edge of the rings. Slide a length of yarn between the rings and tie it very tightly with a knot to hold all the strands together.

4 Remove the rings of the pompom maker and fluff up the pompom. You can trim any straggly ends with scissors to make a neat ball.

CHAPTER 1
Getting Started

The most brilliant thing about knitting is that once you have learned the basics, the rest falls into place quite nicely. So, if you can cast on and bind (cast) off and make knit and purl stitches, then you're ready to go. The projects in this section are all fairly small—or knitted on large needles—so are quick to complete. Have a flick through, get your needles and yarn sorted—and get clicking.

Bunting

These days, bunting isn't just for street parties and big outdoor occasions—you can use it to celebrate whatever you want, in your own home. This easy-to-knit bunting is the perfect way for newbie knitters to make their mark on the world of interior decorating. Go pastel sweet as shown here, or choose your own riot of colors. Go short, go long—the decision is entirely down to you.

Yarn and other materials

Sublime Baby Cashmere Merino Silk DK (75% extra fine merino wool, 20% silk, 5% cashmere) light worsted (DK) yarn
• 1 x 1¾ oz/50 g ball (127 yd/116 m) each of 195 Puzzle, 162 Pinkaboo, 048 Cheeky (A)
Patons Diploma Gold DK (55% wool, 25% acrylic, 20% nylon) light worsted (DK) yarn
• Small amount of 6142 Cream (B)

Needles and equipment
• Size US 3 (3.25 mm) knitting needles
• Yarn sewing needle
• Size G6 (4 mm) or similar size crochet hook
• Small safety pin

Gauge (tension)
27 sts and 36 rows in stockinette (stocking) stitch to a 4-in. (10-cm) square on US 3 (3.25 mm) needles.

Measurements
• Each pennant measures 4 in. (10 cm) from base to tip.

• The bunting has 9 pennants threaded on a 60-in. (1.5-m) cord.

Abbreviations
See page 11.

Bunting
PENNANT
(make 3 in each color A)
Cast on 26 sts.
Knit 4 rows.
Row 5: K2, p to last 2 sts, k2.
Row 6: K.
Row 7: K2, p to last 2 sts, k2.
Row 8: K1, ssk, k to last 3 sts, k2tog, k1. (24 sts)
Row 9: K2, p to last 2 sts, k2.
Row 10: K.
Row 11: K2, p to last 2 sts, k2.
Rep Rows 8–11 twice more. (20 sts)
Row 20: K1, ssk, k to last 3 sts, k2tog, k1. (18 sts)
Row 21: K2, p to last 2 sts, k2.
Rep Rows 20–21 six times more. (6 sts)
Row 34: K1, ssk, k2tog, k1. (4 sts)
Row 35: K.
Row 36: Ssk, k2tog. (2 sts)

Row 37: K.
Row 38: K2tog. (1 st)
Break yarn and pull through rem st.

CORD
Using the crochet hook and B, make a 60-in. (1.5-m) crochet chain.

Making up and finishing

• Weave in loose yarn tails at the tips of the Pennants and the ends of the crocheted Cord.

• With the RS of the Pennants facing, fold over the base of each Pennant to the WS and oversew in place using matching color A to form the casing for the Cord.

• Using the safety pin, thread the Cord through the casings of the Pennants, alternating colors as you go. Spread the Pennants out evenly on the Cord, leaving sufficient length free at each end for hanging up your bunting.

Mug Cozy

Keep your drinks warmer for longer by knitting a cozy for your favorite mug. This is an ideal project if you're just learning how to work cable stitches—so impressive and so much easier than they look. We finished our cozy off with a little strap that slots through the handle, but you could leave it unadorned if you prefer; it'll look great either way.

Yarn and other materials

SMC Select Extra Soft Merino (100% wool) light worsted (DK) yarn
• 1 x 1¾ oz/50 g ball (142 yd/130 m) of 5168 Grass

• ¾ in. (18 mm) pale blue button
• Standard white sewing thread

Needles and equipment
• Size US 8 (5 mm) knitting needles
• Medium cable needle
• Yarn sewing needle
• Standard sewing needle

Gauge (tension)
20 sts and 26 rows in stockinette (stocking) stitch to a 4-in. (10-cm) square on US 8 (5 mm) needles, using yarn double.

Measurements
To fit an average size mug (¾ pint or 360 ml) with straight sides.

Abbreviations
See page 11.

Cozy
(make 1)
Cast on 17 sts using yarn double.
K 2 rows.
Row 3: K1, p3, k9, p3, k1.
Row 4: K4, p9, k4.
Rep last 2 rows 3 times more.
Row 11: K1, p3, k3, C6F, p3, k1.
Row 12: K4, p9, k4.
Row 13: K1, p3, k9, p3, k1.
Row 14: K4, p9, k4.
Row 15: K1, p3, C6B, k3, p3, k1.
Row 16: K4, p9, k4.
Row 17: K1, p3, k9, p3, k1.
Row 18: K4, p9, k4.
Rep Rows 11–18 five times more.
K 3 rows.
Bind (cast) off.

Handle strap
(make 1)
Cast on 7 sts, using yarn double.
K 6 rows.
Row 7: K3, bind (cast) off 2 sts, K to end.
Row 8: K3, turn work and cast on 2 sts, turn back again and k to end.
Row 9: K.
Bind (cast) off.

Making up and finishing
• Fold the Cozy in half widthways and sew up ⅜ in. (1 cm) with mattress stitch (see page 23) at the top and bottom of each edge, leaving a large gap in the center for the mug handle. For a snug fit, you may want to try the cozy on your mug, because the position of the handle may vary slightly.
• Lay the Strap over the handle gap with the flat end on the right. Overstitch the flat end in place. Sew the button in position to match the buttonhole.

Coat Hanger Covers

Why hang your favorite outfits on boring old coat hangers, when with a small amount of yarn and a bit of imagination you can hang them on a coat hanger with its very own knitted cover? As well as looking gorgeous, these knitted covers will make sure your best dress does not slip off the hanger in your closet and become damaged!

Yarn and other materials

FOR THE STRIPED COVER:

Debbie Bliss Cashmerino DK (55% merino wool, 33% microfiber, 12% cashmere) light worsted (DK) yarn
• 1 x 1¾ oz/50 g ball (120 yd/110 m) of 042 Rose Pink (A)

Rowan Cashsoft DK (57% extra fine merino, 33% microfiber, 10% cashmere) light worsted (DK) yarn
• 1 x 1¾ oz/50 g ball (125 yd/115 m) of 509 Lime (B)

FOR THE CABLE STITCH COVER:

SMC Extra Soft merino (100% merino wool) light worsted (DK) yarn
• 1 x 1¾ oz/50 g ball (142 yd/130 m) of 5165 Lime Green (C)

Needles and equipment

• Size US 3 (3.25 mm) knitting needles
• Small or medium cable needle (for cable stitch cover)
• Yarn sewing needle
• 2 x 17 in. (43 cm) wooden coat hangers

Gauge (tension)

20 sts and 48 rows in garter stitch and 25 sts and 36 rows in cable stitch pattern to a 4-in. (10-cm) square on US 3 (3.25 mm) needles.

Measurements

To fit standard wooden coat hangers measuring 17 in. (43 cm) across.

Abbreviations

See page 11.

Striped cover

COVER

(make 1)
Cast on 18 sts in A.
Rows 1–6: K.
Leave A at side and join in B.
Rows 7–8: K.
Rep last 8 rows 18 times more.
K 6 rows in A.
Bind (cast) off.

POMPOM TRIM

Make 2 pompoms in B (see page 25), each approx. 1¼ in. (3 cm) in diameter. Braid (plait) three lengths of yarn to make a 4¾-in. (12-cm) length of cord. Fasten a pompom to each end of the cord.

Cable stitch cover

(make 1)
Cast on 19 sts in C.
Row 1: P3, k4, p5, k4, p3.
Row 2: K3, p4, k5, p4, k3.
Row 3: P3, C4F, p5, C4F, p3.
Row 4: K3, p4, k5, p4, k3.
Rep last 4 rows 33 times more.
Bind (cast) off.

Making up and finishing

• Fold the knitted strips in half lengthways with RS out and join one of the short ends and half of the long seam using mattress stitch (see page 23) and matching yarn.
• Put the Cover over the hanger, carefully taking the hook through a gap between stitches in your knitting.
• Complete the long seam and the second short seam using mattress stitch. Wrap the pompom trim round the striped coat hanger.

Potholder

Add a touch of retro charm to your kitchen with this charming potholder. Knitted quite tightly in a chunky wool yarn in the palest of blues, it offers excellent protection from those hot pot handles. It will look good, too, hanging in your kitchen. The potholder is an excellent project if you're **new** to knitting—especially if you're the sort of person who wants something practical as well as decorative.

Yarn and other materials

Rowan Big Wool (100% wool) chunky yarn
• 1 x 3½ oz/100 g ball (87 yd/80 m) of 021 Ice Blue

NEEDLES AND EQUIPMENT
• Size US 8 (5 mm) knitting needles
• Yarn sewing needle

Gauge (tension)

14 sts and 22 rows in main pattern to a 4-in. (10-cm) square on US 8 (5 mm) needles.

Measurements

The potholder measures 8¾ in. (22 cm) square, excluding loop.

Abbreviations

See page 11.

Potholder

MAIN PIECE
(make 1)
Cast on 33 sts.
K 4 rows.
Row 5: K6, [p1, k1, p1, k3] to last 3 sts, k3.
Row 6: K3, p4, k1, [p5, k1] to last 7 sts, p4, k3.
Rep last 2 rows 19 times more.
Row 45: K6, [p1, k1, p1, k3] to last 3 sts, k3.
K 3 rows.
Bind (cast) off.

LOOP
(make 1)
Cast on 22 sts.
Bind (cast) off.

Making up and finishing

• Use the two yarn tails on the Loop to sew it to one corner of the Main Piece. Weave in any other yarn ends.

Striped Pillow

With some chunky pure wool yarn and a pair of big knitting needles, you can create a sophisticated pillow cover in no time. The cover features some simple but lovely textures and is made from three rectangles, with no tricky fastenings. There is a simple vent at the back for inserting your pillow form (and removing it if you want to wash the cover) and it is finished off with natural mother-of-pearl buttons for that extra touch of class.

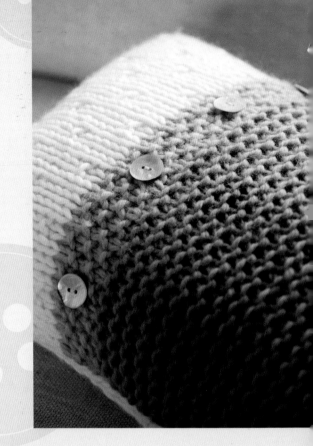

Yarn and other materials
Rowan Big Wool (100% wool) chunky yarn
- 2 x 3½ oz/100 g balls (174 yd/160 m) of 061 Concrete (A)
- 1 x 3½ oz/100 g ball (87 yd/80 m) each of 068 Sun (B), 001 White Hot (C)

- 4 x ¾ in (2 cm) mother-of-pearl buttons
- Standard white sewing thread
- 12 x 20 in. (30 x 50 cm) pillow form

Needles and equipment
- Size US 10½ (6.5 mm) knitting needles
- Yarn sewing needle
- Standard sewing needle

Gauge (tension)
11 sts and 16 rows in stockinette (stocking) stitch to a 4-in. (10-cm) square on US 10½ (6.5 mm) needles.

Measurements
To fit a 12 x 20 in. (30 x 50 cm) pillow form.

Abbreviations
See page 11.

Pillow cover
FRONT
(make 1)
Cast on 33 sts in A.
Rows 1–60: K.
Break A and join in B.
Row 61: K.
Row 62: K1, [p1, k1] to end.
Rep last row 4 times more.
Break B and join in C.
Work 2 rows in st st beg with a k row.
Row 69: K4, [p1, k3] to last st, k1.
Work 3 rows in st st beg with a p row.
Row 73: K2, [p1, k3] to last 3 sts, p1, k2.
Work 3 rows in st st beg with a p row.
Rep last 8 rows once more.
Row 85: K4, [p1, k3] to last st, k1.
Work 3 rows in st st beg with a p row.
Bind (cast) off.

BACK
PIECE 1
(make 1)
Cast on 33 sts in B.
Work 38 rows in st st beg with a k row.
Bind (cast) off

PIECE 2
(make 1)
Cast on 33 sts in C.
Work 37 rows in st st beg with a k row.
Next row: K.
Bind (cast) off.

Making up and finishing

• Lay the Front RS down. Lay the Piece 1 RS up on the WS of the Front and join along the three matching edges using mattress stitch (see page 23) and A. With the Front still RS down, lay Piece 2 on top so it overlaps Piece 1 across the middle of the pillow cover to form a flap to insert the pillow form. Sew Piece 2 to the Front along the three matching edges using mattress stitch.

• Sew the buttons in place along the stripe in B on the front of the pillow. Insert the pillow form.

Phone Cozy

This phone cozy can also be used for MP3/MP4 players to protect your gadget when you're on the go. It's designed to fit snugly—there are no fiddly fastenings to undo so you won't miss important calls. The simple cable pattern makes it a great first project to take that first step up from simple plain and purl knitting.

Yarn and other materials

Patons Diploma Gold DK (55% wool, 25% acrylic, 20% nylon) light worsted (DK) yarn
• 1 x 1¾ oz/50 g ball (131 yd/120 m) of 6220 Blue

Needles and equipment

• Size US 3 (3.25 mm) knitting needles
• Small or medium cable needle

Gauge (tension)

24 sts and 36 rows in stockinette (stocking) stitch to a 4-in. (10-cm) square on US 3 (3.25 mm) needles.

Measurements

To fit a phone or MP3/MP4 player approx. 4¾–5 in. (12–12.5 cm) high and 2½ in. (6.5 cm) wide.

Note

To adapt the pattern for devices around 4½ in. (11.5 cm) high and 2½ in. (6.5 cm) wide, omit Rows 31–36.

Abbreviations

See page 11.

Cozy

FRONT/BACK
(make 2 the same)
Cast on 19 sts.
Row 1: P6, k1, [p1, k1] 3 times, p6.
Row 2: K6, p1tbl, [k1, p1tbl] 3 times, k6.
Rep last 2 rows once more.
Row 5: P6, slip next 4 sts onto cable needle and leave at back of work, k1, p1, k1, then p1, k1, p1, k1 from cable needle, p6.
Row 6: K6, p1tbl, [k1, p1tbl] 3 times, k6.
Row 7: P6, k1, [p1, k1] 3 times, p6.
Row 8: K6, p1tbl, [k1, p1tbl] 3 times, k6.
Rep last 2 rows once more.
Rows 11–30: Rep Rows 1–10 twice more.
Rows 31–36: Rep Rows 1–6 once more.
Row 37: [K1, p1] to last st, k1.
Row 38: [P1, k1] to last st, p1.
Rows 39–40: Rep Rows 37–38.
Bind (cast) off keeping to the k1, p1 pattern.

Making up and finishing

• Join the two side seams using the flat seam technique (see page 23). With the cozy RS together, oversew the bottom seam. Turn the cozy RS out.

Tablet Cozy

Keep your treasured tablet safe and sound in its own stripy home. This is one of the simplest projects in the book to knit, and an ideal second or third project for the newbie knitter. As a bonus, it is also very straightforward to seam together. Why not make it as a gift in the colors of the lucky recipient's favorite sports team?

Yarn and other materials

Rowan Wool Cotton DK (50% merino wool, 50% cotton) light worsted (DK) yarn
• 1 x 1¾ oz/50 g ball (123.5 yd/113 m) each of 943 Flower (A) and 946 Elf (B)

• 1 in. (2.5 cm) green button

Needles and equipment

• Size US 8 (5 mm) knitting needles
• Yarn sewing needle

Gauge (tension)

15 sts and 24 rows in stockinette (stocking) stitch to a 4-in. (10-cm) square on US 8 (5 mm) needles, using yarn double.

Measurements

Laid flat the case measures 7¾ x 10 in. (19.5 x 25 cm), to fit a tablet measuring approx. 7¼ x 9½ in. (18.5 x 24 cm). The case will fit the tablet quite snugly, which will help keep it secure.

Abbreviations

See page 11.

Cozy

FRONT/BACK

(make 2 the same)
Cast on 32 sts in A, using yarn double.
Rows 1–6: Work in st st beg with a k row. Leaving A at side, join in a doubled strand of B.
Rows 7–8: Work in st st beg with a k row. Rep last 8 rows 5 times more.
Fasten off B.
Work 2 rows in st st using A.
Row 51: [K2, p2] to end.
Rep last row twice more.
Bind (cast) off kwise.

FLAP

Cast on 32 sts in A, using yarn double.
Row 1: K.
Row 2: K3, p to last 3 sts, k3.
Rep last 2 rows 3 times more.
Row 9: K1, k2tog, k to last 3 sts, ssk, k1. (30 sts)
Row 10: K3, p to last 3 sts, k3.
Row 11: K.
Row 12: K3, p to last 3 sts, k3.
Row 13: K1, k2tog, k to last 3 sts, ssk, k1. (28 sts)

Row 14: K1, k2tog, k9, bind (cast) off 4 sts (for the buttonhole), k to last 3 sts, ssk, k1. (22 sts)
Row 15: K1, k2tog, k8, turn work and cast on 4 sts (for the buttonhole), turn work again, k to last 3 sts, ssk, k1. (24 sts)
Row 16: K1, k2tog, k to last 3 sts, ssk, k1. (22 sts)
Bind (cast) off.

Making up and finishing

• With WS together, join the Front and Back of the cozy together at the sides using mattress stitch (see page 23) and A. Oversew the lower seam from the inside. From the outside, oversew the Flap in place along the top of the back.
• Sew the button in place using a separated strand of B.

Heart Garland

A knitted garland of pink and red hearts is a romantic new take on traditional bunting. The hearts are knitted entirely in garter stitch and involve only a small amount of shaping—which makes this a great project for the new or intermediate knitter.

Yarn and other materials

Debbie Bliss Rialto DK (100% extra fine merino wool) light worsted (DK) yarn
• 1 x 1¾ oz/50 g ball (114.5 yd/105 m) of 12 Scarlet (A)

Sublime Baby Cashmere Merino Silk DK (75% extra fine merino wool, 20% silk, 5% cashmere) light worsted (DK) yarn
• 1 x 1¾ oz/50 g ball (126 yd/116 m) of 048 Cheeky (B)

Sirdar Country Style DK (40% nylon, 30% wool, 30% acrylic) light worsted (DK) yarn
• 1 x 1¾ oz/50 g ball (170 yd/155 m) of 393 Rustic Pink (C)

• 6 yd/5.5 m of yarn B for the cord
• Approx. ¾ oz (20 g) fiberfill toy filling

Needles and equipment
• Size US 5 (3.75 mm) knitting needles
• Yarn sewing needle

Gauge (tension)
24 sts and 40 rows in garter stitch to a 4-in. (10-cm) square on US 5 (3.75 mm) needles.

Measurements
Each heart measures approx. 3 in. (8 cm) tall and 2½ in. (6 cm) wide. The finished garland measures 1¾ yd (1.6 m).

Note
Make three hearts in yarn A, three in B, and three in C.

Abbreviations
See page 11.

Heart

FRONT/BACK
(make 2 the same)
Cast on 2 sts in A, B, or C.
Row 1: [Inc1] twice. (4 sts)
K 3 rows.
Row 5: K1, M1, k2, M1, k1. (6 sts)
K 3 rows.
Row 9: K1, M1, k to last st, M1, k1. (8 sts)
K 3 rows.
Rep last 4 rows three times more. (14 sts)
K 4 rows.
Row 29: K7, turn work.
Row 30: K7.
Row 31: K2tog, k3, ssk. (5 sts)
Row 32: K2tog, k1, ssk. (3 sts)

Row 33: S1, k2tog, psso. (1 st)
Break yarn and pull through rem st.
Rejoin yarn to center of work.
K 2 rows.
Row 31: K2tog, k3, ssk. (5 sts)
Row 32: K2tog, k1, ssk. (3 sts)
Row 33: S1, k2tog, psso. (1 st)
Break yarn and pull through rem st.

Making up and finishing
• Place two matching heart pieces RS together and oversew round the edges with matching yarn, leaving a 1-in. (2.5-cm) gap at one side for turning and stuffing. Turn the heart the RS out, stuff lightly, and stitch the gap closed.
• Cut three 2-yd (1.8-m) lengths of B. Knot the three lengths together at one end and make a 1¾-yd (1.6-m) braid (plait). Thread the unknotted length of the braided (plaited) cord through the top of the hearts, alternating the three colors. Knot the end and distribute the hearts evenly along the cord, leaving enough cord at each end to hang the garland up.

TIP
You can easily make the
garland longer or shorter by
knitting more or fewer hearts
and varying the length of
the cord.

Lacy Scarf

When the nights start drawing in and the mercury in the thermometer slides downward, it is surely time to knit yourself a new scarf. This scarf is knitted in a beautifully light natural yarn. The simple lace rib pattern is stunning—and once you get into the swing of it, it is also amazingly simple and satisfying.

Yarn and other materials
Rowan Alpaca Cotton (72% alpaca, 28% cotton) worsted (Aran) yarn
• 1 x 1¾ oz/50 g ball (148 yd/135 m) of 400 Rice

Needles and equipment
• Size US 8 (5 mm) knitting needles
• Yarn sewing needle

Gauge (tension)
12½ sts and 14 rows in pattern to a 4-in. (10-cm) square on US 8 (5 mm) needles.

Measurements
The scarf measures 6¼ x 52¾ in. (16 x 134 cm).

Abbreviations
See page 11.

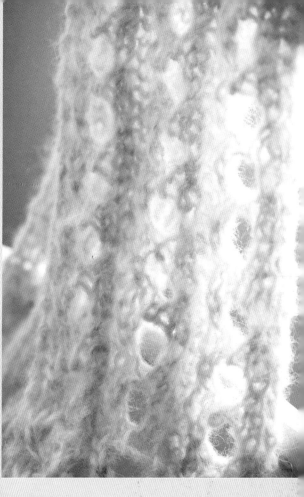

Scarf

Cast on 20 sts.

Row 1: *P2, k2tog, [yo twice], ssk; rep from * to last 2 sts, p2.

Row 2: K2, *p1, k1, p2, k2; rep from * to end.

Row 3: *P2, k4; rep from * to last 2 sts, p2.

Row 4: K2, *p4, k2; rep from * to end.

Rep last 4 rows 46 times more.

Bind (cast) off loosely.

Making up and finishing

• Weave in loose ends.

Yarn and other materials

Sirdar Country Style DK (40% nylon, 30% wool, 30% acrylic) light worsted (DK) yarn

- 1 x 1¾ oz/50 g ball (170 yd/155 m) of 409 Naturelle (MC)
- Very small amount of 395 Anthracite (A)
- Very small amount of 418 Garnet (B)

Debbie Bliss Baby Cashmerino (55% merino wool, 33% microfiber, 12% cashmere) yarn

- Very small amount of 032 Sky (C)

- 2 x 4 in. (5 x 10 cm) rectangle of plain white or cream cheesecloth or fine cotton
- ¼–½ oz (10 g) fiberfill toy filling
- Small handful of dried lavender

Needles and equipment

- Size US 3 (3.25 mm) knitting needles
- Yarn sewing needle
- Large-eyed embroidery needle
- Standard sewing needle and white or cream sewing thread

Gauge (tension)

24 sts and 32 rows in stockinette (stocking) stitch to a 4-in. (10-cm) square on US 3 (3.25 mm) needles.

Measurements

The owl is approx. 4 in. (10 cm) tall.

Abbreviations

See page 11.

Owl Lavender Bag

This wise little owl, with his simple textured front, will keep your linens smelling floral-fresh or would make an excellent stocking filler or small gift. Tuck among your small clothing items or add a loop of ribbon if you want your ornithological lavender bag to adorn a coat hanger.

Owl

BACK

(make 1)

Cast on 14 sts in MC.

Row 1: Inc1, k to last 2 sts, inc1, k1. (16 sts)

Row 2: P.

Row 3: K2, M1, k to last 2 sts, M1, k1. (18 sts)

Row 4: P.

Rep last 2 rows once more. (20 sts)*

Work 20 rows in st st beg with a k row.

Row 27: K2, k2tog, k to last 4 sts, ssk, k2. (18 sts)

Work 3 rows in st st beg with a p row.

Row 31: K2, k2tog, k to last 4 sts, ssk, k2. (16 sts)

Row 32: P.

Row 33: K2, k2tog, k to last 4 sts, ssk, k2. (14 sts)

Row 34: K.

Row 35: K2, M1, k to last 2 sts, M1, k2. (16 sts)

Bind (cast) off kwise.

FRONT

(make 1)

Work as for Back until *.

Row 7: K7, p6, k7.

Row 8: P.

Row 9: K6, p8, k6.

Row 10: P.

Row 11: K5, p10, k5.

Row 12: P.

Rep last 2 rows 3 times more.

Row 19: K6, p8, k6.

Row 20: P.

Row 21: K7, p6, k7.

Row 22: P.

Row 23: K8, p4, k8.

Work 3 rows in st st beg with a p row.

Row 27: K2, k2tog, k to last 4 sts, ssk, k2. (18 sts)

Work 3 rows in st st beg with a p row.

Row 31: K2, k2tog, k to last 4 sts, ssk, k2. (16 sts)

Row 32: P.

Row 33: K2, k2tog, k to last 4 sts, ssk, k2. (14 sts)

Row 34: K.

Row 35: K2, M1, k to last 2 sts, M1, k2. (16 sts)

Bind (cast) off kwise.

Making up and finishing

• With Back and Front WS together, join the sides of the owl using mattress stitch (see page 23) and MC, leaving a gap at the side for stuffing. Oversew the lower seam from the inside and the top seam from the outside.

• Fold the rectangle of fabric in half widthwise and sew the two side seams. Fill with lavender and then stitch the top closed.

• Stuff the owl with fiberfill, inserting the lavender bag inside, then stitch the gap closed.

• Using C, work two sets of Lazy Daisy Stitch (see page 25) for the eyes.

• Using B, work a French Knot (see page 25) in the center of each eye for the pupil. Using A, work two sets of Straight Stitch, one over the other, to form a V-shape for the beak.

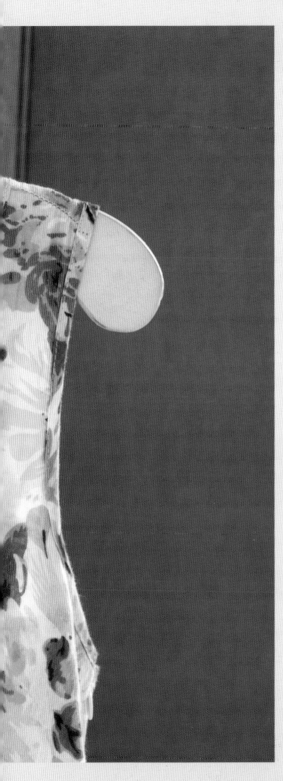

Clutch Bag

This super-easy clutch bag is knitted all in one piece in a gentle shade of pink. The sweet little bow is simple to make from just two small strips of knitting and the optional wrist strap is even more straightforward to put together. The bag is just the right size to hold all the essentials for an evening out. And once you've knitted it, you'll want to knit one to match every outfit in your wardrobe!

Yarn and other materials
Katia Maxi Merino (55% merino, 45% acrylic) chunky yarn
• 1 x 3½ oz/100 g ball (137 yd/ 125 m) of shade 26 (A)
• Small amount of shade 03 (B)

• ⅝ in. (1.5 cm) snap fastener

Needles and equipment
• Size US 8 (5 mm) knitting needles
• Yarn sewing needle

Gauge (tension)
16 sts and 24 rows in stockinette (stocking) stitch to a 4-in. (10-cm) square on US 8 (5 mm) needles.

Measurements
The bag is 7 in. (18 cm) wide and 4½ in. (11 cm) tall (excluding strap).

Abbreviations
See page 11.

Bag

Cast on 26 sts in A.

Row 1: K.

Work 4 rows in st st beg with a k row.

Row 6: K2, M1, k to last 2 sts, M1, k2. (28 sts)

Work 3 rows in st st beg with a p row.

Rep last 4 rows twice more. (32 sts)

Work 6 rows in st st beg with a k row.

Row 24: K2, k2tog, k to last 4 sts, ssk, k2. (30 sts)

Row 25: P2tog, p to last 2 sts, p2tog. (28 sts)

Row 26: K2, M1, k to last 2 sts, M1, k2. (30 sts)

Row 27: P.

Rep last 2 rows once more. (32 sts)

Work 8 rows in st st beg with a k row.

Row 38: K2, k2tog, k to last 4 sts, ssk, k2. (30 sts)

Work 3 rows in st st beg with a p row.

Rep last 4 rows once more. (28 sts)

Row 46: K2, k2tog, k to last 4 sts, ssk, k2. (26 sts)

Work 2 rows in st st beg with a p row.

Row 49: K2, p to last 2 sts, k2.

Row 50: K.

Row 51: K2, p to last 2 sts, k2.

Rep last 2 rows 4 times more.

Row 60: K2, k2tog, k to last 4 sts, ssk, k2. (24 sts)

Row 61: K2, p to last 2 sts, k2.

Rep last 2 rows once more. (22 sts)

Row 64: K2, k2tog, k to last 4 sts, ssk, k2. (20 sts)

Row 65: K2tog, k to last 2 sts, ssk. (18 sts)

Rep last row once more. (16 sts)

Bind (cast) off kwise.

Bow

LOOP

Cast on 40 sts in B.

Work 4 rows in st st beg with a k row.

Bind (cast) off pwise.

CENTER

Cast on 8 sts in B.

Work 2 rows in st st beg with a k row.

Bind (cast) off pwise.

Wrist strap

Cast on 40 sts in A.

Bind (cast) off.

Making up and finishing

• Fold the cast-on edge upward to form the main part of the bag and sew the side seams using mattress stitch (see page 23). Fold down the bound-(cast-)off edge of the bag to form the top flap. Using yarn, sew the snap fastener in position. Sew the Wrist strap to one side of the bag.

• For the bow, sew the short edges of the Loop piece together. Wrap the bow Center round the Loop piece and secure it at the back. The seam of the Loop piece should now be concealed. Sew the bow to the bag.

Pencil Pot

If you're tired of seeing pens and pencils lying around, now is the time to knit them their very own home. This simple pot, worked in an easy textured stitch, is an ideal first or second project for new knitters. Once you've mastered the basics, you'll easily be able to work out how to knit these useful containers in different sizes to suit all your storage needs!

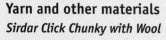

Yarn and other materials

Sirdar Click Chunky with Wool
(70% acrylic, 30% wool) chunky yarn
• 1 x 1¾ oz/50 g ball (82 yd/75 m)
of 146 Bloom (A)
Rowan Pure Wool DK (100% wool) light worsted (DK) yarn
• Small amount of 030 Damson (B)

Needles and equipment

• Size US 6 (4 mm) knitting needles
• Yarn sewing needle

Gauge (tension)

18 sts and 32 rows in seed (moss) stitch to a 4-in. (10-cm) square using A on US 6 (4 mm) needles.

Measurements

The pencil pot is 4¼ in. (11 cm) tall.

Abbreviations

See page 11.

Pot

SIDES
(make 1)
Cast on 54 sts in A.
Row 1: [K1, p1] to end.

Row 2: [P1, k1] to end.
Rep these 2 rows 16 times more.
Break yarn and join in B, using yarn double.
Next row: K.
Bind (cast) off.

BASE
(make 1)
Cast on 14 sts in A.
Row 1: [K1, p1] to end.
Row 2: [P1, k1] to end.
Rep last 2 rows 11 times more.
Bind (cast) off.

Making up and finishing

• Turn Sides piece so it is WS outward. Using A, join the short edges together using mattress stitch (see page 23).
• Place the Base in position on the bottom of the Sides so that the back seam of the Sides is in the center of the bound-(cast-) off edge of the Base. Oversew right around all the edges of the Base from the inside to secure it to the Sides.

CHAPTER 2
Getting Better

Now you will be totally confident with basic knitting techniques, including easy shaping and piecing your work together. And you just know it's tIme to try something a little different—perhaps more unusual stitch combinations or some new techniques. But don't panic—all the patterns in this section are still quite straightforward and, as always, the patterns include full instructions on what you need to do.

Wash Cloths

These pretty wash cloths are knitted in a beautifully soft pure cotton yarn using a simple lacy stitch. They are an ideal first project if you're just learning to knit lace because there is no shaping or any fancy edges. Cotton yarns come in some beautiful colors, so knit a batch for your kitchen or bathroom and you will never want to use a boring old flannel again.

Yarn and other materials
Sublime Egyptian Cotton DK
(100% cotton) light worsted (DK) yarn
• 1 x 1¾ oz/50 g ball (115 yd/105 m) in each of 329 Cornelia, 328 Freya (A)

Needles and equipment
• Size US 5 (3.75 mm) knitting needles
• Yarn sewing needle

Gauge (tension)
19 sts and 25 rows in lace pattern to a 4-in. (10-cm) square on US 5 (3.75 mm) needles.

Measurements
Each wash cloth measures 11 in. (28 cm) square.

Abbreviations
See page 11.

Cloth
(make 1)
Cast on 57 sts in (A).
K 4 rows.
Row 5: K5, [yo, s1, k2tog, psso, yo, k1] to last 4 sts, k4.
Row 6: K3, p to last 3 sts, k3.
Row 7: K4, k2tog, yo, k1 [yo, s1, k2tog, psso, yo, k1] to last 6 sts, yo, s1, k1, psso, k4.
Row 8: K3, p to last 3 sts, k3.
Rep last 4 rows 15 times more.
K 4 rows.
Bind (cast) off.

Making up and finishing
• Weave in all loose ends.

Hot Water Bottle Cover

In a world of high-tog duvets and electric blankets, there's still nothing like a snug hot water bottle to keep your feet balmy on winter nights. The cover is knitted in a bright blue super chunky yarn—so it knits up in a jiffy. And if you're new to knitted motifs, this simple heart is a great first project. The cover features a roll neck top, so you can fill your bottle without removing it—a great advantage when you're ready for bed and every second counts.

Yarn and other materials

Sirdar Big Softie (51% wool, 49% acrylic) chunky yarn
- 2 x 1¾ oz/50 g balls (98 yd/90 m) of 343 Puffball (A)
- 1 x 1¾ oz/50 g ball (49 yd/45 m) of 330 Meringue (B)

- 3 x ¾ in. (2 cm) mother-of-pearl buttons
- Standard cream sewing thread

Needles and equipment

- Size US 10½ (6.5 mm) knitting needles
- Yarn sewing needle
- Standard sewing needle

Gauge (tension)

10 sts and 16 rows in stockinette (stocking) stitch to a 4-in. (10-cm) square on US 10½ (6.5 mm) needles.

Measurements

The cover will fit a standard hot water bottle measuring approx. 7½ x 13 in. (19 x 33 cm).

Abbreviations

See page 11.

Front

(make 1)
Cast on 19 sts in A.
Row 1: Inc1, k to last 2 sts, inc1, k1. (21 sts)
Row 2: P.
Rep last 2 rows once more. (23 sts)
Work 8 rows in st st beg with a k row.
Row 13: K11 in A, join in B and k1 in B, k in A to end.
Row 14: P10 in A, p3 in B, p in A to end.
Row 15: K10 in A, k3 in B, k in A to end.
Row 16: P9 in A, p5 in B, p in A to end.
Row 17: K9 in A, k5 in B, k in A to end.
Row 18: P8 in A, p7 in B, p in A to end.
Row 19: K8 in A, k7 in B, k in A to end.
Row 20: P7 in A, p9 in B, p in A to end.
Row 21: K7 in A, k9 in B, k in A to end.
Row 22: P6 in A, p11 in B, p in A to end.
Row 23: K6 in A, k11 in B, k in A to end.
Rep last 2 rows once more.
Row 26: P6 in A, p11 in B, p in A to end.
Row 27: K6 in A, k5 in B, k1 in A (using A from separate ball), k5 in B, k in A to end.
Row 28: P6 in A, p5 in B, p1 in A, p5 in B, p in A to end.
Row 29: K7 in A, k3 in B, k3 in A, k3 in

B, k in A to end.
Row 30: P7 in A, p3 in B, p3 in A, p3 in B, p in A to end.
Cont in A only.
Work 8 rows in st st beg with a k row.
Row 39: K1, k2tog, k to last 3 sts, ssk, k1. (21 sts)
Row 40: P.
Row 41: Bind (cast) off 5 sts, k to end. (16 sts)
Row 42: Bind (cast) off 5 sts pwise, p to end. (11 sts)
Row 43: K1, [p1, k1] to end.
Row 44: P1, [k1, p1] to end.

Rep last 2 rows 10 times more.
Bind (cast) off keeping to the k1, p1 pattern.

Back
LOWER BACK
(make 1)
Cast on 19 sts in A.
Row 1: Inc1, k to last 2 sts, inc1, k1. (21 sts)
Row 2: P.
Rep last 2 rows once more. (23 sts)
Work 16 rows in st st beg with a k row.
Row 21: K1, [p1, k1] to end.
Rep last row 3 times more.
Bind (cast) off kwise.

UPPER BACK
Cast on 23 sts in A.
Row 1: K1, [p1, k1] to end.
Row 2: K1, p1, k1, lift last but 1 st over last st, p1, [k1, p1] 4 times, lift last but 1 st over last st, [k1, p1] 4 times, k1, lift last but 1 st over last st, p1, k1. (20 sts)
Row 3: K1, p1, M1, [p1, k1] 4 times, M1, [k1, p1] 4 times, M1, p1, k1. (23 sts)
Row 4: K1, [p1, k1] to end.
Work 14 rows in st st beg with a k row.
Row 19: K1, k2tog, k to last 3 sts, ssk, k1. (21 sts)
Row 20: P.
Row 21: Bind (cast) off 5 sts, k to end. (16 sts)
Row 22: Bind (cast) off 5 sts pwise, p to end. (11 sts)
Row 23: K1, [p1, k1] to end.
Row 24: P1, [k1, p1] to end.
Rep last 2 rows 10 times more.
Bind (cast) off keeping to the k1, p1 pattern.

Making up and finishing
• Place the Lower Back and Front pieces WS together and sew the side seams using mattress stitch (see page 23).
• Place the Upper Back piece in position and sew the side seams using mattress stitch.
• Turn the cover WS out and oversew the lower seam and the shoulder seams. Sew the ribbing section using mattress stitch from the WS, as this section will fold down on the finished item.
• Sew buttons in position on the back.

Cottage Doorstop

Why use an ordinary old doorstop when you can knit yourself a pretty little cottage? Knitted in two strands of light worsted (DK) yarn, the cottage comes together much more quickly than you'd think. We've chosen to knit our cottage in cream—but it would also work well in white, pale yellow, or pastel pink.

TIP
If you're feeling adventurous, why not try making the variation doorstop on page 63?

Yarn and other materials

Patons Diploma Gold DK (55% wool, 25% acrylic, 20% nylon) light worsted (DK) yarn
• 1 x 1¾ oz/50 g ball (131 yd/120 m) of 6142 Cream (A)

Sublime Baby Cashmere Merino Silk DK (75% extra fine merino wool, 20% silk, 5% cashmere) light worsted (DK) yarn
• 1 x 1¾ oz/50 g ball (126 yd/116 m) of 220 Froggie (B)

Debbie Bliss Rialto DK (100% extra fine merino wool) light worsted (DK) yarn
• Small amount of 12 Scarlet (C)

Rowan Pure Wool DK (100% wool) light worsted (DK) yarn
• Very small amount of 019 Avocado (D)

• 3–4 small decorative buttons
• Approx. 2½ cups (8 oz/500 g) rice or dried lentils
• Medium size polythene bag
• Approx. 2 oz (50 g) fiberfill toy filling
• Small amounts of light turquoise (E) and yellow (F) light worsted (DK) yarns (for variation)

Needles and equipment
• Size US 8 (5 mm) knitting needles
• Yarn sewing needle
• Large-eyed embroidery needle
• Water-erasable pen
• Size US 2/3 (3 mm) knitting needles (for variation)

Gauge (tension)
18 sts and 26 rows in stockinette (stocking) stitch to a 4-in. (10-cm) square on US 8 (5 mm) needles, using yarn double.

Measurements
The doorstop is 6½ in. (16.5 cm) high.

Abbreviations
See page 11.

Cottage
FRONT/BACK PANEL
(make 2 the same)
Cast on 22 sts in A, using yarn double.
Work 14 rows in st st beg with a k row.
Row 15: K1, k2tog, k to last 3 sts, ssk, k1. (20 sts)
Work 9 rows in st st beg with a p row.
Row 25: K1, k2tog, k to last 3 sts, ssk, k1. (18 sts)
Row 26: P.
Fasten off A and join double strand of B.
K 2 rows.
Work 2 rows in st st beg with a k row.
K 2 rows.

Rep last 4 rows once more.
Row 37: K1, k2tog, k to last 3 sts, ssk, k1. (16 sts)
Row 38: P.
K 2 rows.
Bind (cast) off.

SIDE PANEL
(make 2 the same)
Cast on 16 sts in A, using yarn double.
Work 14 rows in st st beg with a k row.
Row 15: K1, k2tog, k to last 3 sts, ssk, k1. (14 sts)
Work 9 rows in st st beg with a p row.
Row 25: K1, k2tog, k to last 3 sts, ssk, k1. (12 sts)
Row 26: P.
Fasten off A and join double strand of B.
K 2 rows.
Work 2 rows in st st beg with a k row.
K 2 rows.
Rep last 4 rows once more.
Row 37: K1, k2tog, k to last 3 sts, ssk, k1. (10 sts)
Row 38: P.
K 2 rows.
Bind (cast) off.

BASE
(make 1)
Cast on 22 sts in A, using yarn double.
Work 20 rows in st st beg with a k row.
Bind (cast) off.

TOP
(make 1)
Cast on 16 sts in B, using yarn double.
Work 12 rows in st st beg with a k row.
Bind (cast) off.

Strap

(make 1)

Cast on 4 sts in B, using yarn double.

K 22 rows.

Bind (cast) off.

Making up and finishing

• Using A, sew one Side panel
to each side of one of the Front/Back
panels with mattress stitch (see page
23). Sew the second Front/Back panel
to one of the Side panels, again using
mattress stitch. From the inside, oversew
the Base in place along four sides and
oversew two sides of the Top in place.

• Put the rice or dried lentils into the
polythene bag and insert into the
doorstop. Fill the remainder of the
doorstop with fiberfill toy filling and
stitch the remaining two sides
of the Top. Oversew the ends of the
Strap in place.

• Mark the position of windows and door
using the water-erasable pen. Using B,
work the window frame and cross bars in
Straight Stitch (see page 24). Using C,
work the door outline in Chain Stitch
(see page 24). Using D, work the stems
of flowers in Straight Stitch. Stitch on
buttons for the flowers.

Variation

Make up the cottage and strap as before,
then knit the windows and door as follows:

Windows

(make 2)

Cast on 7 sts in E.

Work 7 rows in st st beg with a k row.

Bind (cast) off.

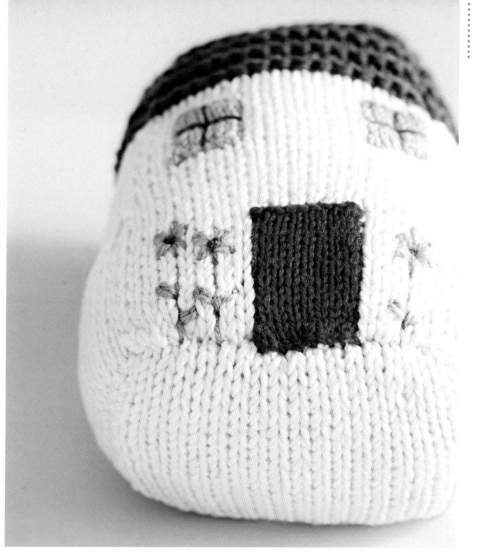

Door

(make 1)

Cast on 8 sts in C.

Work 15 rows in st st beg with a k row.

Bind (cast) off kwise.

Making up and finishing

• Oversew windows and doors in place
using matching yarns.

• Using B, work four Straight Stitches
from the center of the window to the
mid-point of each side. Using F, work the
flowers in Lazy Daisy Stitch (see page
24). Using B, work French Knots (see

page 24) for the flower centers. Using D,
work each flower stem in Straight Stitch
and each leaf in a single Lazy Daisy Stitch.

Woodland Key Rings

Conjure up a fairytale key ring in virtually no time—you can buy split key rings from most craft stores and the only other items you need are scraps of yarn and the odd button. We can't guarantee it will work magic, but the toadstool is not poisonous and the colorful flower is charming.

Yarn and other materials

Debbie Bliss Rialto DK (100% extra fine merino wool) light worsted (DK) yarn
• 1 x 1¾ oz/50 g ball (114.5 yd/105 m) of 12 Scarlet (A)

Sublime Cashmere Merino Silk DK (75% extra fine merino wool, 20% silk, 5% cashmere) light worsted (DK) yarn
• Very small amount of 223 Latte (B)

Rowan Pure Wool DK (100% wool) light worsted (DK) yarn
• Small amount of 019 Avocado (C)

Sublime Extra Fine Merino Wool DK (75% extra fine merino wool, 20% silk, 5% cashmere) light worsted (DK) yarn
• 1 x 1¾ oz/50 g ball (126 yd/116 m) of 306 Petticoat (D)

• Standard white and cream sewing thread
• Small amount of fiberfill toy filling
• 7 tiny white buttons
• ⅝ in. (1.5 cm) red button
• Split key rings

Needles and equipment
• Size US 3 (3.25 mm) knitting needles
• Yarn sewing needle
• Standard sewing needle

Gauge (tension)
24 sts and 32 rows in stockinette (stocking) stitch to a 4-in. (10-cm) square on US 3 (3.25 mm) needles.

Measurements
• The toadstool measures 2½ in. (6 cm) in diameter.
• The flower measures 2¼ in. (5.5 cm) in diameter.

Abbreviations
See page 11.

Toadstool
CAP
(make 1)
Cast on 48 sts in A.
Work 7 rows in st st beg with a k row.
Row 8: [P2tog] to end. (24 sts)

Row 9: K.
Row 10: [P2tog] to end. (12 sts)
Break yarn, thread through rem sts,
pull up tightly, and secure.

STALK AND GILLS

(make 1)
Cast on 48 sts in B.
Row 1: K.
Row 2: [P2tog] to end. (24 sts)
Row 3: K.
Row 4: [P2tog] to end. (12 sts)
Work 10 rows in st st beg with a k row.
Bind (cast) off.

HANGING CORD

(make 1)
Cast on 24 sts in C.
Bind (cast) off.

HANGING CORD

(make 1)
Cast on 24 sts in A.
Bind (cast) off.

Making up and finishing

• Fold the toadstool Cap in half widthwise with RS together and oversew the back seam using A. Fold the Stalk and Gills in half widthwise with RS together and oversew the lower and back seam using B. Turn both pieces RS out. Oversew the outer edge of Gill section to underside of Cap, just inside from edge, leaving a gap for stuffing. Stuff quite firmly and sew the gap closed. Using white thread, sew white buttons onto the cap. Sew the hanging cord in place and thread the free end onto the split key ring.

• Fold the Leaf pieces in half widthwise with WS together and oversew round edges using C. Fold the Petal strip in half lengthwise with WS together so holes along the middle form a wavy edge. Oversew along lower edge using D. Fold back 1 in. (2.5 cm) along one short edge of Petal piece and oversew along bottom. Fold the remainder of the Petal strip around the folded part, oversewing in place as you go. Sew the Leaves in place. Using cream thread, sew the button in the center of the flower. Sew the hanging cord in place and thread the free end onto the split key ring.

Flower
PETALS

(make 1)
Cast on 60 sts in D.
Work 6 rows in st st.
Row 7: K2, [yo twice, k2tog twice] to last 2 sts, yo twice, k2. (62 sts)
Row 8: P.
Row 9: K1, [yo, k2tog] to last st, yo, k1. (63 sts)
Work 5 rows in st st beg with a p row.
Bind (cast) off.

LEAVES

(make 2)
Cast on 2 sts in C.
Row 1: [Inc1] twice. (4 sts)
Row 2: P.
Row 3: Inc1, k1, inc1, k1. (6 sts)
Work 7 rows in st st beg with a p row.
Row 11: K2tog, k2, ssk. (4 sts)
Row 12: P.
Row 13: K2tog, ssk. (2 sts)
Row 14: P2tog. (1 st)
Break yarn and pull through rem st.

Bolster

At the end of the day when you want to settle into your favorite seat and put your feet up, this bolster cushion is the icing on the cake. Knitted in a retro-style wave pattern, it's a great first project for knitters getting used to working with two colors at a time—and the super chunky yarn and super chunky needles to match mean it will be ready in almost no time.

Yarn and other materials

Rowan Big Wool (100% merino wool) chunky yarn
• 1 x 3½ oz/100 g ball (87 yd/80 m) in each of 036 Glamour (A), 064 Prize (B), 068 Sun (C), 001 Hot White (D)

• 18 in. (46 cm) x 8 in. (20 cm) diameter bolster pillow form

Needles and equipment
• Size US 10½ (6.5 mm) knitting needles
• Yarn sewing needle

Gauge (tension)
12 sts and 15 rows in stockinette (stocking) stitch to a 4-in. (10-cm) square on US 10½ (6.5 mm) needles.

Measurements
To fit an 18 in. (46 cm) x 8 in. (20 cm) diameter bolster pillow form.

Abbreviations
See page 11.

Main piece
(make 1)
Cast on 71 sts in A.
Work 6 rows in st st beg with a k row.
Row 7: K1 in B, [k4 in A, k1 in B] to end.
Row 8: P1 in B, [p4 in A, p1 in B] to end.
Row 9: K2 in B, [k2 in A, k3 in B] to last 4 sts, k2 in A, k2 in B.
Break A.
Work 3 rows in st st beg with a p row.
Row 13: K1 in C, [k4 in B, k1 in C] to end.
Row 14: P1 in C, [p4 in B, p1 in C] to end.
Row 15: K2 in C, [k2 in B, k3 in C] to last 4 sts, k2 in B, k2 in C.
Break B.
Work 3 rows in st st beg with a p row.
Row 19: K1 in D, [k4 in C, k1 in D] to end.
Row 20: P1 in D, [p4 in C, p1 in D] to end.
Row 21: K2 in D, [k2 in C, k3 in D] to last 4 sts, k2 in C, k2 in D.
Break C.
Cont in D only.

Beg with a p row, cont in st st until work measures 17¾ in. (45 cm), ending with a p row.
Bind (cast) off.

End pieces
(make 2)
Cast on 12 sts in D.
Row 1: Inc1, k to last st, inc1, k1. (14 sts)
Row 2: P.
Rep last 2 rows 4 times more. (22 sts)
Work 10 rows in st st beg with a k row.
Row 21: K1, k2tog, k to last 3 sts, ssk, k1. (20 sts)
Row 22: P.
Rep last 2 rows 3 times more. (14 sts)
Row 29: K1, k2tog, k to last 3 sts, ssk, k1. (12 sts)
Bind (cast) off pwise.

Making up and finishing
• Join seam of Main Piece using mattress stitch (see page 23), leaving a 7-in. (17.5-cm) gap in the center for inserting the pillow form. From the RS, join the End Pieces in place using mattress stitch so that the cast-on and bound-(cast-)off edges of the main piece form a narrow border round the circumference of the end pieces.
• Insert the pillow form and close the gap using mattress stitch.

Bath Mat

If you're fed up with run-of-the-mill bath mats, then this project is a must-do. This super soft mat is knitted in a mega chunky yarn that contains both cotton and wool, so it is cozy and absorbent too. If you want your work to be on permanent show, rather than hanging over the edge of your bath tub, it would also make a lovely bedside rug to keep your toes cozy as you get up to face the day.

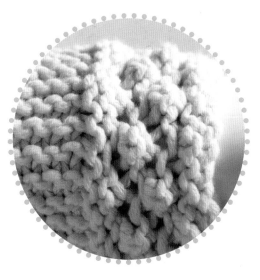

Yarn and other materials
Sirdar Denim Ultra (60% acrylic, 25% cotton, 15% wool) chunky yarn
• 3 x 3½ oz/100 g balls (246 yd/225 m) of 508 Ivory Cream

Needles and equipment
• Size US 15 (10 mm) knitting needles
• Yarn sewing needle

Gauge (tension)
9 sts and 17 rows in garter st to a 4-in. (10-cm) square on US 15 (10 mm) needles.

Measurements
The mat measures 18½ x 24 in. (47 x 61 cm).

Abbreviations
See page 11.

Bath mat
CENTER PANEL
Cast on 30 sts.
K 80 rows.
Bind (cast) off.

SIDE BORDERS
With RS facing, pick up and k 42 sts along one (row edge) side of work.
Row 1: K.
Row 2: P.
Row 3: K1, *[k1, p1, k1] into next st, p3tog; rep from * to last st, k1.
Row 4: P.
Row 5: K1, *p3tog, [k1, p1, k1] into next st; rep from * to last st, k1.
Row 6: P.
Row 7: K1, *[k1, p1, k1] into next st, p3tog; rep from * to last st, k1.
Row 8: P.
Bind (cast) off.
Rep border along the other (row edge) side.

TOP/BOTTOM BORDER
With RS facing, pick up and k 42 sts along top edge, including the side borders just worked.
Row 1: K.
Row 2: P.
Row 3: K1, *[k1, p1, k1] into next st, p3tog; rep from * to last st, k1.
Row 4: P.
Row 5: K1, *p3tog, [k1, p1, k1] into next st; rep from * to last st, k1.
Row 6: P.
Row 7: K1, *[k1, p1, k1] into next st, p3tog; rep from * to last st, k1.
Row 8: P.
Bind (cast) off.
Rep border along bottom edge.

Making up and finishing
• Weave in any loose yarn tails.

Egg Cozies

Cheer up your eggs at breakfast time with this trio of quirky egg cozies. Choose your own colors to transform this into a great yarn stash-busting project—or follow the colors we've used here. The cozies are very quick to make as an ideal small Easter gift for friends and family.

Yarn and other materials

FOR THE BLUEBIRD EGG COZY:
Debbie Bliss Baby Cashmerino (55% merino wool, 33% microfiber, 12% cashmere) yarn
- 1 x 1¾ oz/50 g ball (137 yd/125 m) of 204 Baby Blue (A)
- Very small amounts of deep yellow (B) and black (C) light worsted (DK) yarns

FOR THE FRENCHMAN EGG COZY:
Rowan Pure Wool DK (100% wool) light worsted (DK) yarn
- 1 x 1¾ oz/50 g ball (137 yd/125 m) of 036 Kiss (A)

Sirdar Country Style DK (40% nylon, 30% wool, 30% acrylic) light worsted (DK) yarn
- 1 x 1¾ oz/50 g ball (170 yd/155 m) of 409 Naturelle (B)

Rowan Cashsoft DK (10% merino wool, 57% acrylic, 33% microfiber) light worsted (DK) yarn
- 1 x 1¾ oz/50 g ball (126 yd/115 m) of 535 Blue Jacket (C)
- Very small amounts of black (D) and dusky pink (E) light worsted (DK) yarns

FOR THE BLONDE GIRL EGG COZY:
Patons Diploma Gold DK (55% wool, 25% acrylic, 20% nylon) light worsted (DK) yarn
- 1 x 1¾ oz/50 g ball (131 yd/120 m) of 6243 Bright Aqua (A)

Sirdar Country Style DK (40% nylon, 30% wool, 30% acrylic) light worsted (DK) yarn
- 1 x 1¾ oz/50 g ball (170 yd/155 m) of 409 Naturelle (B)

Debbie Bliss Baby Cashmerino (55% merino wool, 33% microfiber, 12% cashmere) yarn
- 1 x 1¾ oz/50 g ball (137 yd/125 m) of 060 Hot Pink (C)

Sirdar Click Chunky (70% acrylic, 30% wool) chunky yarn
- Small amount of 186 Lemon (D)
- Very small amounts of black (E) and red (F) light worsted (DK) yarns

Needles and equipment
- Size US 3 (3.25 mm) knitting needles
- Yarn sewing needle
- Large-eyed embroidery needle
- Red coloring pencil

Gauge (tension)
25 sts and 28 rows to a 4-in. (10-cm) square on US 3 (3.25 mm) needles.

Measurements
All the egg cozies are 2¾ in. (7 cm) tall.

Abbreviations
See page 11.

Row 8: K1, p2, k1.
Row 9: K2tog, ssk. (2 sts)
Row 10: K2tog.
Break yarn and pull rem st through.

BEAK
(make 1)
Cast on 7 sts in B.
Bind (cast) off.

Making up and finishing

• Join the back seam of the cozy using mattress stitch (see page 23). Oversew the wings in position. Fold the beak in half widthwise and oversew it in place.
• Work two French Knots (see page 24) in C for the eyes.

Frenchman
(make 1)
Cast on 42 sts in A.
Row 1: K.
Work 4 rows in st st beg with a k row.
Break A and join in B.
Work 12 rows in st st beg with a k row.
Break B and join in C.
Work 4 rows in st st beg with a k row.
Row 22: K2, [s1, k2tog, psso, k4] 5 times, s1, k2tog, psso, k2. (30 sts)
Row 23: P.
Row 24: K1, [s1, k2tog, psso, k2] 5 times, s1, k2tog, psso, k1. (18 sts)
Row 25: P2tog to end. (9 sts)
Row 26: [S1, k2tog, psso] 3 times. (3 sts)
Work 3 rows in st st beg with a p row.
Bind (cast) off.

Bluebird
MAIN COZY
(make 1)
Cast on 42 sts in A.
Row 1: K.
Work 20 rows in st st beg with a k row.
Row 22: K2, [s1, k2tog, psso, k4] 5 times, s1, k2tog, psso, k2. (30 sts)
Row 23: P.
Row 24: K1, [s1, k2tog, psso, k2] 5 times, s1, k2tog, psso, k1. (18 sts)

Row 25: P2tog to end. (9 sts)
Thread yarn through rem sts, pull up tightly, and secure.

WINGS
(make 2)
Cast on 6 sts in A.
Row 1: K.
Row 2: K1, p to last st, k1.
Rep last 2 rows twice more.
Row 7: K1, k2tog, ssk, k1. (4 sts)

Break B and join in C.

K 2 rows.

Work 4 rows in st st beg with a k row.

Row 22: K2, [s1, k2tog, psso, k4] 5 times, s1, k2tog, psso, k2. (30 sts)

Row 23: P.

Row 24: K1, [s1, k2tog, psso, k2] 5 times, s1, k2tog, psso, k1. (18 sts)

Row 25: P2tog to end. (9 sts)

Trim yarn, thread through rem sts, and secure.

Making up and finishing

• Join the back seam of the cozy using mattress stitch (see page 23) and matching yarns.

• Work two French Knots (see page 24) in E for the eyes. Separate a strand of E and work three Straight Stitches (see page 24) above each eye for the eyelashes. Using a separated strand of F, work two Straight Stitches in a flat V-shape for the mouth.

• For the hair, cut six 10-in. (25-cm) lengths of D and divide the lengths into two groups each consisting of three lengths. Secure the center of each group to the side of the cozy, just under the "hat." Braid (plait) the yarn lengths and secure the ends.

• Use the red coloring pencil to color the cheeks.

Making up and finishing

• Join the back seam of the cozy using mattress stitch (see page 23) and matching yarns.

• Work two French Knots (see page 24) in D for the eyes. Separate a strand of D and work two Straight Stitches (see page 24) for the eyebrows. Use another single strand of D to work the moustache in Chain Stitch (see page 24). Using E, work two small Straight Stitches, one over the other, for the mouth.

• Use the red coloring pencil to color the cheeks.

Blonde Girl

(make 1)

Cast on 42 sts in A.

Row 1: K.

Work 4 rows in st st beg with a k row.

Break A and join in B.

Work 10 rows in st st beg with a k row.

Napkin Rings

Jazz up your dining table and impress your friends with these funky floral napkin rings. The main napkin ring is knitted in a textured seed (moss) stitch and the flowers are much easier to work than they look. This project is an ideal way of using up your stash—and they are so quick to make you'll be able to knit enough to adorn your table in just a few evenings.

Yarn and other materials

Rowan Cashsoft DK (10% merino wool, 57% acrylic, 33% microfiber) light worsted (DK) yarn
• Small amount of 509 Lime (A)
Sirdar Country Style DK (40% nylon, 30% wool, 30% acrylic) light worsted (DK) yarn
• Small amount of 604 Damson (B)
Sublime Baby Cashmere Merino Silk DK (75% merino, 20% silk, 5% cashmere) light worsted (DK) yarn
• Small amount of 001 Piglet (C)

• ½ in. (11 mm) green button
• ½ in. (11 mm) yellow button

Needles and equipment

• Size US 2/3 (3 mm) knitting needles
• Yarn sewing needle
• Large-eyed embroidery needle

Gauge (tension)

28 sts and 30 rows in seed (moss) stitch to a 4-in. (10-cm) square on US 2/3 (3 mm) needles.

Measurements

The napkin rings measure approx. 1¾ in. (4.5 cm) in diameter.

Abbreviations

See page 11.

Ring

(make one)
Cast on 11 sts in A or B.
Row 1: K1, [p1, k1] to end.
Rep last row 43 times more.
Bind (cast) off.

Flower

(make 1)
Cast on 10 sts in B or C.
Row 1: Inc1 twice.
Turn and work on 4 sts just knitted only.
Work 11 rows in st st beg with a p row.
Next row: K2tog, ssk, lift RH st over LH st. (1 st)
*Next row: K1 into next cast-on st, inc1.
Turn and work on 4 sts just worked only.
Work 11 rows in st st beg with a p row.
Next row: K2tog, ssk, lift RH st over LH st.** (1 st)

Rep from * to ** 3 more times.
K into first cast-on st to complete final petal. (2 sts)
Bind (cast) off 1 st, break yarn, and pull through rem st.

Making up and finishing

• Join the back seam of the Ring using mattress stitch (see page 23) and matching yarn.
• Stitch the Flower in B on the Ring in A and the Flower in C on the Ring in B.
• Using the large-eyed embroidery needle, stitch the green button on the C Flower using A and the yellow button on the B Flower using C.

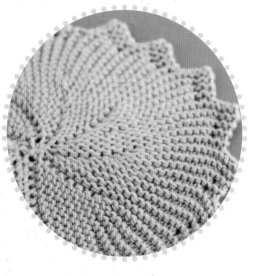

Placemats

Have you ever been irritated to discover that no shop seems to stock placemats in the color you need? Well now you can knit your own placemats in any shade you want—to match your own décor and crockery or those of the lucky recipient. These easy-to-knit round mats with a lace edge are simple enough for almost all knitters—but interesting enough to keep you on your toes.

Yarn and other materials

Sublime Baby Cashmere Merino Silk DK (75% extra fine merino wool, 20% silk, 5% cashmere) light worsted (DK) yarn
• 1 x 1¾ oz/50 g ball (127 yd/116 m) each of 124 Splash (A) and 162 Pinkaboo (B)

Needles and equipment

• Size US 8 (5 mm) knitting needles
• Yarn sewing needle

Gauge (tension)

16 sts and 28 rows in garter stitch to a 4-in. (10-cm) square on US 8 (5 mm) needles using yarn double.

Measurements

The placemat measures approx. 12 in. (30 cm) in diameter.

Abbreviations

See page 11:

Placemat

Cast on 20 sts in A or B.
Row 1: K.
Row 2 (RS): K2, yo, k17, turn (1 st rem on LH needle).
Row 3: S1, k to end. (21 sts)
Row 4: K2, yo, k17, turn (2 sts rem on LH needle).
Row 5: S1, k to end. (22 sts)
Row 6: K2, yo, k17, turn (3 sts rem on LH needle).
Row 7: S1, k to end. (23 sts)
Row 8: K2, yo, k17, turn (4 sts rem on LH needle).
Row 9: S1, K to end. (24 sts)
Row 10: Bind (cast) off 4 sts (1 st rem on RH needle), k1, yo, k13, turn (5 sts rem on LH needle).
Row 11: S1, k to end. (21 sts)
Row 12: K2, yo, k13, turn (6 sts rem on LH needle).
Row 13: S1, k to end. (22 sts)
Row 14: K2, yo, k13, turn (7 sts rem on LH needle).
Row 15: S1, k to end. (23 sts)
Row 16: K2, yo, k13, turn (8 sts rem on LH needle).

Row 17: S1, k to end. (24 sts)
Row 18: Bind (cast) off 4 sts, k to end. (20 sts)
Rep last 18 rows 7 times more.
Row 1: K.
Row 2 (RS): K2, yo, k17, turn. (1 st rem on LH needle)
Row 3: S1, k to end. (21 sts)
Row 4: K2, yo, k17, turn. (2 sts rem on LH needle)
Row 5: S1, k to end. (22 sts)
Row 6: K2, yo, k17, turn. (3 sts rem on LH needle)
Row 7: S1, k to end. (23 sts)
Row 8: K2, yo, k17, turn. (4 sts rem on LH needle)
Row 9: S1, k to end. (24 sts)
Row 10: Bind (cast) off 4 sts (1 st rem on RH needle), k1, yo, k13, turn. (5 sts rem on LH needle)
Row 11: S1, k to end. (21 sts)
Row 12: K2, yo, k13, turn. (6 sts rem on LH needle)
Row 13: S1, k to end. (22 sts)
Row 14: K2, yo, k13, turn. (7 sts rem on LH needle)
Row 15: S1, k to end. (23 sts)

Row 16: K2, yo, k13, turn. (8 sts rem on LH needle)
Row 17: S1, k to end. (24 sts)
Bind (cast) off.

Making up and finishing
• Join the cast-on and bound-(cast-)off edges of the placemat using flat stitch (see page 23).
• Soak mat thoroughly in lukewarm water, squeeze out excess, shape mat, and dry flat.

Fingerless Mitts

When the weather turns chilly, but you still need your fingers free for all those essential tasks, fingerless gloves are the perfect solution. These no-nonsense mitts—with just a hint of lacy interest on the knuckles—are knitted in a cheerful shade of pink. We've given them a nice trim in zingy lime but they would work equally well if knitted plain—the choice is yours.

Yarn and other materials

Sirdar Country Style DK (40% nylon, 30% wool, 30% acrylic) light worsted (DK) yarn
• 1 x 1¾ oz/50 g ball (170 yd/155 m) of 527 Rosehip (A)
Rowan Cashsoft DK (57% extra fine merino, 33% microfiber, 10% cashmere) light worsted (DK) yarn
• Small amount of 509 Lime (B)

Needles and equipment
• Size US 5 (3.75 mm) knitting needles
• Yarn sewing needle
• Stitch holder

Gauge (tension)
24 sts and 28 rows in stockinette (stocking) stitch to a 4-in. (10-cm) square on US 5 (3.75 mm) needles.

Measurements
Each glove measures 2¾ x 6¾ in. (7.5 x 17 cm) when flat and unstretched. To fit an average teenage girl or woman's hand.

Abbreviations
See page 11.

Mitts
(make 2 the same)
Cast on 36 sts in A.
Row 1: [K2, p2] to end.
Rep last row 11 times more.
Work 12 rows in st st beg with a k row.
Row 25: K16, M1, k4, M1, k16. (38 sts)
Next and every WS row: P.
Row 27 (RS): K16, M1, k6, M1, k16. (40 sts)
Row 29: K16, M1, k8, M1, k16. (42 sts)
Row 31: K16, M1, k10, M1, k16. (44 sts)
Row 33: K16, M1, k12, M1, k16. (46 sts)
Row 35: K16, M1, k14, M1, k16. (48 sts)
Row 37: K17, k next 14 sts and put on stitch holder, k to end. (34 sts)
Work 6 rows in st st beg with a p row across all 34 sts.
Row 44: K.
Row 45: K1, [yo, k2tog, k1] to end.
Row 46: K.
Work 2 rows in st st beg with a k row.
Break A and join in B.

Row 49: K.
Bind (cast) off kwise.
Join A to RS of work for thumb sts on stitch holder
Work 5 rows in st st beg with a k row.
Bind (cast) off kwise.

Making up and finishing
• Fold each mitten piece in half with RS together and oversew the thumb seams.
• Turn each mitten RS out and join the main seams using mattress stitch (see page 23).

Storage Basket

There is always something that could do with its very own basket to keep things neat and tidy. It could be socks or handkerchiefs... or it could be your knitting yarn. This gorgeous storage basket is knitted in a mega-chunky yarn in a soft shade of cream with a deep blackcurrant color trim. We've added some felted flowers for fun—but the basket is also lovely just left as it is.

Yarn and other materials
Sirdar Big Softie (51% wool, 49% acrylic) chunky yarn
- 3 x 1¾ oz/50 g balls (147 yd/135 m) of 330 Meringue (A)
- 1 x 1¾ oz/50 g ball (49 yd/45 m) of 324 Fripp (B)

Twilleys Freedom (100% wool) chunky yarn
- Small amount in each of 435 Bluebell (C) and 420 Olive (D)
- Small amount of deep yellow light worsted (DK) yarn (E)

- Standard cream sewing thread

Needles and equipment
- Size US 10 (6 mm) knitting needles
- Yarn sewing needle
- Large-eyed embroidery needle
- Standard sewing needle
- Washing machine (for felting flowers)

Gauge (tension)
12 sts and 16 rows in stockinette (stocking) stitch to a 4-in. (10-cm) square on US 10 (6 mm) needles.

Measurements
The storage basket measures 9 in. (23 cm) in diameter and is 6¾ in. (17 cm) high.

Abbreviations
See page 11.

Basket
SIDES
(make 1)
Cast on 87 sts in A.
Row 1: P3, [k1, p3] to end.
Row 2: K3, [p1, k3] to end.
Rep last 2 rows 10 times more.
Row 23: P3, [k1, p3] to end.
Break A and join in B.
Work 10 rows in st st beg with a k row.
Bind (cast) off.

BASE
(make 1)
Cast on 14 sts in A.
Row 1: Inc1, k to last 2 sts, inc1, k1. (16 sts)
Row 2: P.
Rep last 2 rows 4 times more. (24 sts)

Work 8 rows in st st beg with a k row.
Row 19: K2tog, k to last 2 sts, ssk. (22 sts)
Row 20: P.
Rep last 2 rows 3 times more. (16 sts)
Row 27: K2tog, k to last 2 sts, ssk. (14 sts)
Bind (cast) off kwise (on WS of work).

Flowers
(make 3)
Cast on 6 sts in C.
Row 1: Bind (cast) off 5 sts.
Row 2: Cast on 5 sts.
Row 3: Bind (cast) off 5 sts.
Rep last 2 rows twice more.

Row 8: Cast on 5 sts.
Bind (cast) off.

Leaves
(make 2)
Leaves are knitted from base to tip.
Cast on 2 sts in D.
Row 1: [Inc1] twice. (4 sts)
Row 2: P.
Row 3: [Inc1, k1] twice. (6 sts)
Work 5 rows in st st beg with a p row.

Row 9: K2tog, k2, ssk. (4 sts)
Row 10: [P2tog] twice. (2 sts)
Row 11: K2tog.
Break yarn and pull through rem st.

Making up and finishing

• Join the two short edges of the Sides using flat stitch (see page 23). Oversew the Sides to the Base from the WS. Turn the basket the RS out. Fold the top edge of the basket in half onto the RS and oversew the bound-(cast-)off edge along the line where the colors change.
• Join the Flower petals into a circle and weave in all yarn tails. Weave in all yarn tails on leaves.
• Wash the Flowers and Leaves in a 104ºF (40ºC) wash to felt the yarn. Reshape while damp and dry thoroughly.
• Using E, embroider a French Knot (see page 24) in the center of each Flower. Using cream thread, stitch the Flowers and Leaves in place on the brim of the basket, using the photograph as a guide.

Grocery Bag Holder

Keep your plastic grocery bags concealed within this knitted holder. Worked in a refreshing shade of lemon, the holder has a hanging handle and an elasticized lower edge to keep your bags in check. It is worked in a very easy basket weave stitch with a simple picot edging. You could leave it plain if you like, in which case it's suitable for novice knitters, but we've made ours look extra decorative with a pair of knitted cherries to give you an extra challenge.

Yarn and other materials

SMC Select Extra Soft Merino (100% merino wool) light worsted (DK) yarn
• 1 x 1¾ oz/50 g ball (142 yd/130 m) of 5118 Lemon (A)

• Small amounts of red (B) and dark green (C) light worsted (DK) yarn
• 8-in. (20-cm) length of narrow elastic tape
• Very small amount of fiberfill toy filling

Needles and equipment
• Size US 5 (3.75 mm) and size US 3 (3.25 mm) knitting needles
• US size G6 (4 mm) crochet hook
• Yarn sewing needle
• Small safety pin

Gauge (tension)
24 sts and 36 rows over pattern to a 4-in. (10-cm) square on US 5 (3.75 mm) needles.

Measurements

The bag holder is approx. 12 in. (30 cm) long, excluding handle.

Abbreviations

See page 11.

Main bag

(make 1)
Using US 5 (3.75 mm) needles, cast on 50 sts in A.
Work 4 rows in st st beg with a k row.
Row 5: K2, [p2, k2] to end.
Row 6: P2, [k2, p2] to end.
Work 2 rows in st st beg with a k row.
Row 9: P2, [k2, p2] to end.
Row 10: K2, [p2, k2] to end.
Work 2 rows in st st beg with a k row.
Rep last 8 rows 11 times more.
Work 3 rows in st st beg with a k row.
Row 104: K1, [yo, k2tog] to last st, k1.
Work 3 rows in st st beg with a p row.
Bind (cast) off.

Handle

(make 1)
Using US 5 (3.75 mm) needles and using A double, cast on 40 sts.
K 4 rows.
Bind (cast) off.

Cherry

(make 2)
Using US 3 (3.25 mm) needles, cast on 4 sts in B.
Row 1: [Inc1] 4 times. (8 sts)
Row 2: P.
Row 3: [Inc1] 8 times. (16 sts)

Work 3 rows in st st beg with a p row.
Row 7: [K2tog] 8 times. (8 sts)
Row 8: P.
Row 9: [K2tog] 4 times. (4 sts)
Thread yarn through rem sts, pull tightly, and secure.

Leaf

(make 2)
Using US 3 (3.25 mm) needles, cast on 2 sts in C.
Row 1: K
Row 2: [Inc1] twice. (4 sts)
Row 3: K.
Row 4: [Inc1, k1] twice. (6 sts)
Row 5: K.
Row 6: Inc1, k3, inc1, k1. (8 sts)
K 6 rows.
Row 13: K2tog, k4, ssk. (6 sts)
Row 14: K.
Row 15: K2tog, k2, ssk. (4 sts)
Row 16: K.
Row 17: K2tog, ssk. (2 sts)
Row 18: K2tog.
Break yarn and pull through rem st.

Stalk

(make 1)
Using the crochet hook, work a 4-in. (10-cm) chain in C.

Making up and finishing

• Sew back seam of Main Bag using mattress stitch (see page 23). Turn up ⅜ in. (1 cm) along lower edge so cast-on edge is visible from RS of holder. Oversew round cast-on edge to form a casing, leaving a small gap for inserting the elastic tape. Use the safety pin to thread the elastic through the casing. Stitch the elastic ends together and then stitch the gap closed. Turn the bound-(cast-)off edge under to form a picot edging and oversew in place.
• Oversew the Handle in place on the inside of the holder.
• Fold each Cherry piece in half with RS on the outside. Join the seam using mattress stitch, stuffing the shape with a small amount of fiberfill as you go. Join the yarn tails at the beginning and end of the Stalk to the top of each cherry. Fasten the center of the stalk and the leaves in place at the top of the holder, using the photograph as a guide.

Coasters

Everyone needs at least one set of coasters to protect those favorite furniture pieces—and what better way to acquire a set than to knit your own? These coasters are a brilliant way of using up odds and ends of light worsted (DK) yarn and a great starter project if you want to try your hand at knitting circles.

Yarn and other materials

Sublime Baby Cashmere Merino Silk DK (75% extra fine merino wool, 20% silk, 5% cashmere) light worsted (DK) yarn
• 1 x 1¾ oz/50 g ball (126 yd/116 m) of 003 Vanilla (A)
• Small amount of 001 Piglet (B)

SMC Select Extra Soft Merino (100% merino wool) light worsted (DK) yarn
• Small amount of 5148 Violet (B)
• 1 x 1¾ oz/50 g ball (142 yd/130 m) ball of 5108 Yellow (A)
• Small amount of 5168 Grass (B)

Rowan Baby Merino Silk DK (66% merino wool, 34% silk) light worsted (DK) yarn
• 1 x 1¾ oz/50 g ball (147 yd/135 m) of 676 Sky (A)

Needles and equipment

• Size US 2/3 (3 mm) knitting needles
• Yarn sewing needle

Row 8: K6, turn. (4 sts left on LH needle)
Row 9: S1, k to end.
Row 10: K5, turn. (5 sts left on LH needle)
Row 11: S1, k to end.
Row 12: K.
Rep last 12 rows 6 times more.
Bind (cast) off.
Using B double, pick up and k 44 sts along outer edge of coaster.
Work 3 rows in st st beg with a p row.
Next row: K2, [yo, k2tog, k1] to end.
Work 2 rows in st st beg with a p row.
Bind (cast) off kwise (on WS of work).

Making up and finishing

• Join the cast-on and bound-(cast-)off edges of the main coaster using flat stitch (see page 23) and join the two short edges of the trim using mattress stitch, so the coaster forms a circle.
• Turn down the long edge of the trim and oversew in place on the underside so that the holes in the trim form a picot edging.
• Soak the coaster thoroughly in lukewarm water, squeeze out excess, shape coaster, and dry flat.

Gauge (tension)

16 sts and 28 rows in garter stitch to a 4-in. (10-cm) square on US 2/3 (3 mm) needles using yarn double.

Measurements

Each finished coaster measures approx. 5¼ in. (13 cm) in diameter.

Abbreviations

See page 11.

Coaster

Cast on 10 sts using A double.
Row 1: K.
Row 2: K9, turn. (1 st left on LH needle)
Row 3: S1, k to end.
Row 4: K8, turn. (2 sts left on LH needle)
Row 5: S1, k to end.
Row 6: K7, turn. (3 sts left on LH needle)
Row 7: S1, k to end.

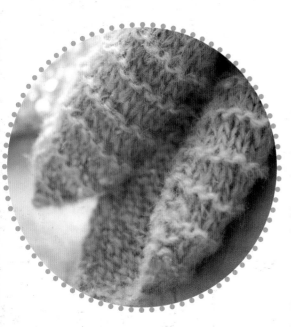

Pull-through Scarf

There's nothing like a scarf to keep you warm when the temperatures take a nose dive—and this sumptuous lacy knit guarantees that you will look glamorous as well as feeling warm and toasty. It's knitted in a really subtle alpaca yarn that suits this lace pattern perfectly—and it's a great place to start if you are new to lacy creations.

Yarn and other materials

Rowan Alpaca Cotton (72% alpaca, 28% cotton) worsted (Aran) yarn

• 1 x 1¾ oz/50 g ball (148 yd/135 m) of 407 Smoked Salmon

• ¾ in. (2 cm) mother-of-pearl button

Needles and equipment

• Size US 8 (5 mm) knitting needles
• Yarn sewing needle
• Stitch holder

Gauge (tension)

15 sts and 25 rows in pattern to a 4-in. (10-cm) square on US 8 (5 mm) needles.

Measurements

The scarf measures 5¼ x 33¾ in. (13 x 86 cm).

Abbreviations

See page 11.

Scarf

Cast on 2 sts.
Row 1: [Inc1] twice. (4 sts)
Row 2: K.
Row 3: [Inc1, k1] twice. (6 sts)
Row 4: K2, p to last 2 sts, k2.
Row 5: Inc1, k to last 2 sts, inc1, k1. (8 sts)
Row 6: K.
Row 7: Inc1, k to last 2 sts, inc1, k1. (10 sts)
Row 8: K2, p to last 2 sts, k2.
Rep last 4 rows once more. (14 sts)
Row 13: Inc1, k to last 2 sts, inc1, k1. (16 sts)
K 2 rows.
Row 16: K2, p to last 2 sts, k2.
Rep last 4 rows twice more. (20 sts)
K 3 rows.
Row 28: K2, p to last 2 sts, k2.
Rep last 4 rows 5 times more.
Row 49: K13, turn.
Row 50: K6, turn work and cont on 6 sts just knitted, leaving rem sts on needles.
K 8 rows.
Break yarn and leave sts just knitted on stitch holder. Rejoin yarn to 7 sts on LH needle on RS of work.
K 3 rows.
Next row: K2, p to end.

K 3 rows.
Next row: K2, p to end.
K 2 rows.
Break yarn and add sts to those already on stitch holder. Rejoin yarn to 7 rem sts on WS of work.
K 2 rows.
Next row: P5, k2.
K 3 rows.
Next row: P5, k2.
K 2 rows.
With RS facing, work across all 20 sts from stitch holder.
Next row: K.
Next row: K2, p to last 2 sts, k2.
K 3 rows.
Next row: K2, p to last 2 sts, k2.
Rep last 4 rows 32 times more.
Next row: K1, k2tog, k to last 3 sts, ssk, k1. (18 sts)
K 2 rows.
Next row: K2, p to last 2 sts, k2.
Rep last 4 rows once more. (16 sts)
Next row: K.
Next row: K1, k2tog, k to last 3 sts, ssk, k1. (14 sts)
Next row: K.
Next row: K1, k2tog, k to last 3 sts, ssk, k1. (12 sts)
Rep last 4 rows once more. (8 sts)

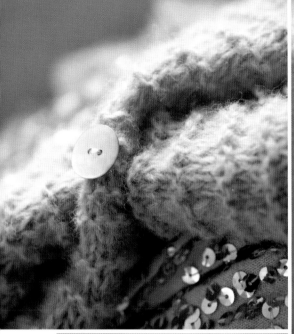

Next row: K.
Next row: K1, k2tog, k2, ssk, k1. (6 sts)
Next row: K.
Next row: K1, k2tog, ssk, k1. (4 sts)
Next row: K.
Next row: K2tog, ssk. (2 sts)
Next row: K2tog. (1 st)
Break yarn and pull through rem st.

Making up and finishing

• Weave in all yarn tails. Sew button
onto top of loop formed by the two slots.

Pencil Case

Create a unique knitted case for your prized writing implements—it is very straightforward to knit although you will need to sew a lining and embroider a few wooly flowers as well. Of course, it docsn't have to be a pencil case—it will also work brilliantly as a make-up bag or just a simple case for keeping all those odds and ends together.

Yarn and other materials

Sirdar Country Style DK (40% nylon, 30% wool, 30% acrylic) light worsted (DK) yarn
• 1 x 1¾ oz/50 g ball (170 yd/155 m) of 399 Honey (MC)

• Very small amounts of bright pink, mid-pink, and turquoise light worsted (DK) yarns
• 3 small buttons in white, pale pink, and pale blue
• 11 x 9 in. (28 x 22 cm) cotton lining fabric
• Standard white and ocher sewing threads
• 7 in. (18 cm) polyester zipper

Needles and equipment

• Size US 8 (5 mm) knitting needles
• Yarn sewing needle
• Large-eyed embroidery needle
• Standard sewing needle

Gauge (tension)

7 sts and 25 rows in stockinette (stocking) stitch to a 4-in. (10-cm) square on US 8 (5 mm) needles, using yarn double.

Measurements

The pencil case measures 3¼ x 7 in. (8 x 18 cm).

Abbreviations

See page 11.

Case

(make 2 the same)
Cast on 32 sts using MC double.
Work 4 rows in st st beg with a k row.
Row 5: Inc1, k to last 2 sts, inc1, k1. (34 sts)
Work 3 rows in st st beg with a p row.
Rep last 4 rows 3 times more. (40 sts)
Bind (cast) off.

Making up and finishing

• Embroider the flowers on one Case piece using Lazy Daisy Stitch (see page 24). Add the button centers.
• Use one knitted piece as a pattern to cut two lining pieces in cotton fabric, adding an extra ⅜ in. (1 cm) all round for the seams.
• Hand stitch the zipper in place between the top edges of both knitted pieces of the Case using a double strand of ocher sewing thread.

• With WS together, join the side and lower seams using mattress stitch (see page 23) and MC.

LINING

• Place the two cotton lining pieces RS together and sew round the two short sides and long side by hand or machine, using a ⅜-in. (1-cm) seam allowance. Turn under ⅜ in (1 cm) round the top edge. Insert the lining into the pencil case With WS together and slip stitch in place along the zipper sides.
• Cut a few short strands of contrast color yarn and thread through the hole in the zip pull. Use another short length of the same yarn to tie the strands together to form a tassel.

Pot Cover

Don't put up with dreary pot covers a moment longer! This delicate pot cover will bring a spark of vintage cheer to any kitchen storage jar—or use it in the bathroom on a jar that stores soaps or cosmetics. It's knitted in two types of easy-to-work lace and finished off with a coordinating cord made from a simple crochet chain.

Yarn and other materials

SMC Select Extra Soft Merino (100% merino wool) light worsted (DK) yarn
• 1 x 1¾ oz/50 g ball (142 yd/130 m) of 5165 Lime Green (A)
• Small amount of 5148 Violet (B)

Needles and equipment

• Size US 2/3 (3 mm) knitting needles
• Size US 7 (4.5 mm) crochet hook
• Yarn sewing needle
• Small safety pin to thread the cord

Gauge (tension)

21 sts and 27 rows in pattern for main section to a 4-in. (10-cm) square on US 2/3 (3 mm) needles.

Measurements

The cover measures approx. 6¼ in. (16 cm) and will fit a jar top approx. 3½ in. (9 cm) in diameter.

Abbreviations

See page 11.

Main cover

Cast on 27 sts in A.
Row 1 (RS): K2 [yo, s1, k2tog, psso, yo, k1] to last st, k1.
Row 2: P.
Row 3: K1, k2tog, yo, k1, [yo, s1, k2tog, psso, yo, k1] to last 3 sts, yo, s1, k1, psso, k1.
Row 4: P.
Rep last 4 rows 9 times more.
Bind (cast) off pwise.

Lace trim

The trim is made separately.

Cast on 7 sts in A.

Row 1: K1, [k2tog, yo twice] twice, k2. (9 sts)

Row 2: K3, [p1, k2] twice.

Row 3: K1, k2tog, yo twice, k2tog, k4.

Row 4: Bind (cast) off 2 sts (1 st rem on RH needle), k3, p1, k2. (7 sts)

Rep last 4 rows 32 times more.

Bind (cast) off.

Cord

Using B double, make a 28-in. (70-cm) crochet chain.

Making up and finishing

• Oversew the Lace Trim to the outer edges of the Main Cover. Join cast-on and bound-(cast-)off edges.

• Weave the yarn tails at each end of the Cord back into itself. Using the small safety pin, thread the cord in and out of the lace pattern, starting at the center of one side, and using the photographs (left) as a guide.

Daisy Book Cover

Protect the book you are reading with your own unique cover. It is knitted in a dense woven pattern that is very easy to get the hang of, after just a few rows. As an added bonus, there is absolutely no shaping! The handy tie-cord will make sure your book stays closed in your purse or bag and the cheerful daisies on the front will lighten even the most somber of tomes!

Yarn and other materials

Debbie Bliss Baby Cashmerino (55% merino wool, 33% microfiber, 12% cashmere) yarn
- 1 x 1¾ oz/50 g ball (137 yd/125 m) of 070 Royal (A)
- Small amounts of white (B) and pale lime green (C) light worsted (DK) yarn

- 8¼ x 11½ in. (21 x 29 cm) of pale pink felt
- Standard sewing thread to match felt
- 3 assorted small yellow buttons

Needles and equipment
- Size US 2/3 (3 mm) knitting needles
- Yarn sewing needle
- US size 7 (4.5 mm) crochet hook
- Large-eyed embroidery needle
- Standard sewing needle

Gauge (tension)
22 sts and 38 rows over main pattern to a 4-in. (10-cm) square on US 2/3 (3 mm) needles.

Measurements
The book cover measures 8¼ x 11⅓ in. (21 x 29 cm) and will fit a standard size paperback book measuring 5 x 7¾ in. (13 x 20 cm) with approx. 200–300 pages.

Abbreviations
See page 11.

Outer cover
(make 1)
Cast on 47 sts in A.
Row 1 (RS): K1, [yfwd, s1 pwise, yb, k1] to end.
Row 2: P.

Row 3: K2, [yfwd, s1 pwise, yb, k1] to last st, k1.
Row 4: P.
Rep last 4 rows 27 times more.
Bind (cast) off.

Flowers
(make 3)
Cast on 6 sts in B.
Row 1: Bind (cast) off 5 sts. (1 st)
Row 2: Cast on 5 sts. (6 sts)
Row 3: Bind (cast) off 5 sts. (1 st)
Rep last 2 rows twice more.
Row 8: Cast on 5 sts. (6 sts)
Bind (cast) off.

Cord
(make 1)
Using the crochet hook and a double strand of C, make a 37-in. (93-cm) crochet chain.
Fasten off.

Making up and finishing
- Using a small running stitch and matching thread, sew the felt to the WS of the Outer cover round the outside edges, about ¼ in. (5 mm) in from the

outside edge, using the photograph (opposite) as a guide.

• Join the Flower petals into a circle at the base and stitch in place. Using a separated strand of C, stitch the buttons in place for the Flower centers.

• Weave the yarn tails of the Cord into itself. With the inside of the Outer Cover facing, stitch the Cord in place on the center of the RH side so the Cord to the right measures 28 in. (70 cm) and the Cord to the left measures 9 in. (23 cm).

• Place your piece of felt on a flat surface so that it is wider than it is tall. Cut two vertical slits in the felt, each one 5 in. (13 cm) in from the short edges. The top and bottom of the slits should be just over ¼ in. (7 mm) from the top and lower edges. (The slits will be used for inserting the covers of your book when your project is finished). Insert the book covers through the long slits in the felt. Close the cover. Wrap the long length of Cord twice round the book clockwise then tie in a bow at the front using the shorter length of Cord.

CHAPTER 3
Now You Are Really Good

The projects in the final part of our collection demand a little more time and, in some cases, include slightly more advanced or unusual techniques. But, by now, these will all be well within your grasp. So curl up on the couch, browse through the final pages, and take your pick.

Tea Light Shade

Transform a simple glass jar into a retro-cool tea light shade with this lacy cream knit. The jar shown here is pink but the shade would work just as well on a plain glass jar. Once you've realized how quick and easy it is to knit the impressive lace, you'll want to make a whole set to brighten winter days and summer evenings.

Yarn and other materials
Patons Diploma Gold DK (55% wool, 25% acrylic, 20% nylon) light worsted (DK) yarn
• 1 x 1¾ oz/50 g ball (131 yd/120 m) of 6142 Cream

• Glass tea light jar measuring approx. 5 in. (12.5 cm) high by 3 in. (7.5 cm) diameter, with wire handle (optional)

Needles and equipment
• Size US 3 (3.25 mm) and size US 6 (4 mm) knitting needles
• Yarn sewing needle

Gauge (tension)
16 sts and 32 rows in main pattern to a 4-in. (10-cm) square on US 6 (4 mm) needles.

Measurements
Because the lacy knit is very stretchy, the shade will fit most standard medium-size jars, up to a maximum of 5 in. (12.5 cm) high by 3 in. (7.5 cm) diameter.

Note
The shade is made by knitting the top band first; the main part of the shade is then knitted onto the top band.

Abbreviations
See page 11.

Shade
TOP BAND
(make 1)
Using US 3 (3.25 mm) needles, cast on 7 sts.
Row 1: K1, [k2tog, yo twice] twice, k2. (9 sts)
Row 2: K3, [p1, k2] twice.
Row 3: K1, k2tog, yo twice, k2tog, k4.
Row 4: Bind (cast) off 2 sts (1 st rem on RH needle), k3, p1, k2. (7 sts)
Rep last 4 rows 15 times more.
Bind (cast) off.

MAIN SHADE
Using US 6 (4 mm) needles, pick up and k 34 sts across straight edge of top edging.
Row 1: K1, *k2tog, yo twice, k2tog; rep from * to last st, k1.
Row 2: P1, *p2, k1, p1; rep from * to last st, p1.
Rep last 2 rows 11 times more.
Bind (cast) off.

Making up and finishing
• Fold the Shade in half widthwise and join the side seam using the flat seam technique (see page 23).

Beehive Tea Cozy

There's nothing quite like a nice cup of tea made in a proper teapot to go with your teatime treats. This unashamedly cutesy tea cozy will be the perfect addition to your vintage-style tea table. We've gone quite over the top with the decoration, but think it would work almost as well with just one or two bees and flowers—so the choice is yours!

Yarn and other materials

Rowan Creative Focus Worsted (75% wool, 25% alpaca) worsted (Aran) yarn
• 1 x 3½ oz/100 g ball (220 yd/200 m) of 2132 Camel (A)

Click Sirdar DK (70% acrylic, 30% wool) light worsted (DK) yarn
• Small amounts of 138 Black (B) and 188 Rustica (C)

Debbie Bliss Angel (76% super kid mohair, 24% silk) laceweight yarn
• Small amount of 01 Angel (D)

Sirdar Country Style DK (40% nylon, 30% wool, 30% acrylic) light worsted (DK) yarn
• Small amount of 527 Rosehip (E)

Rowan Pure Wool DK (100% wool) light worsted (DK) yarn
• Small amount of 019 Avocado (F)

• 6 small mother-of-pearl or white buttons
• Standard cream sewing thread
• Small amount of fiberfill toy filling

Needles and equipment

• Size US 5 (3.75 mm) and size US 2/3 (3 mm) knitting needles
• Size US 7 (4.5 mm) crochet hook
• Stitch holder
• Yarn sewing needle
• Standard sewing needle

Gauge (tension)

20 sts and 26 rows in stockinette (stocking) stitch to a 4-in. (10-cm) square on US 5 (3.75 mm) needles.

Measurements

The cozy measures 8¾ in. (22 cm) wide x 6¾ in. (17 cm) tall when laid flat.
To fit a 6-cup teapot measuring approx. 5½ x 5½ in. (14 x 14 cm).

Abbreviations

See page 11.

Cozy

FIRST PART

*Using size US 5 (3.75 mm) needles, cast on 45 sts in A.

Row 1: K.
Row 2: P.
Row 3: K.
Rep last 3 rows 12 times more.
Row 40: K5, k2tog, k9, k2tog, k9, ssk, k9, ssk, k5. (41 sts)
Row 41: P.
K 2 rows.
Row 44: P4, p2tog, p8, p2tog, p9, p2tog, p8, p2tog, p4. (37 sts)
K 2 rows
Row 47: P.
Row 48: K4, k2tog, k7, k2tog, k7, ssk, k7, ssk, k4. (33 sts)
Break yarn and leave sts on stitch holder.

SECOND PART

Work as First Part from * but do not break yarn.

Row 49: K all sts from Second Part then k all sts from First Part, remembering to k sts from First Part with RS facing. (66 sts)

Row 50: P.

Row 51: K4, [s1, k2tog, psso, k8] 5 times, s1, k2tog, psso, k4. (54 sts)

Row 52: K.

Row 53: P.

Row 54: K.

Row 55: K3, [s1, k2tog, psso, k6] 5 times, s1, k2tog, psso, k3. (42 sts)

Row 56: P.

K 2 rows.

Row 59: P.

Row 60: K.

Row 61: K2, [s1, k2tog, psso, k4] 5 times, s1, k2tog, psso, k2. (30 sts)

Row 62: P.

K 2 rows.

Row 65: P.

Row 66: K.

Row 67: K1, [s1, k2tog, psso, k2] 5 times, s1, k2tog, psso, k1. (18 sts)

Row 68: [P2tog] to end. (9 sts)

Break yarn, thread it through rem sts, pull quite tightly, and secure.

Loop

Using the crochet hook and A double, work a 2½-in. (6-cm) crochet chain.

Bees

BODY

(make 6)

Using US 2/3 (3 mm) needles, cast on 5 sts in B.

Row 1: Inc1, k2, inc1, k1. (7 sts)
Row 2: P.
Leave B at side and join in C.
Row 3: Inc1, k4, inc1, k1. (9 sts)
Row 4: P.
Leave C at side and use B.
Row 5: Inc1, k6, inc1, k1. (11 sts)
Row 6: P.
Work 2 rows in st st using C, beg with a
k row.
Work 2 rows in st st using B, beg with a
k row.
Work 2 rows in st st using C, beg with a
k row.
Break C and work remainder of bee in B.
Row 13: K1, k2tog, k5, ssk, k1. (9 sts)
Row 14: P2tog, p5, p2tog. (7 sts)
Bind (cast) off. Break yarn and pull
through rem st.

WINGS
(make 6)
Using US 2/3 (3 mm) needles, cast on
4 sts in D.
Row 1: Inc1, k1, inc1, k1. (6 sts)
Row 2: Inc1, k3, inc1, k1. (8 sts)
K 8 rows.
Row 11: K2tog, k4, ssk. (6 sts)
Row 12: K2tog, k2, ssk. (4 sts)
Bind (cast) off.

Daisies
(make 6)
Using US 2/3 (3 mm) needles, cast on
6 sts in E.
Row 1: K2, turn and cont working on
these 2 sts only, leaving rem sts on
needle.
*Work 10 rows in st st beg with a p row.

Row 12: Lift RH st over LH st. (1 st)
Pick up and k into cast-on edge at base
to form a loop. (2 sts)
Lift RH st over LH st. (1 st)
Next row: K1 (from sts rem on needle).
(2 sts)**
Rep from * to ** until you have 4 petals.
Work 10 rows in st st beg with a p row.
Next row: Lift RH st over LH st. (1 st)
Pick up and k into cast-on edge to form a
loop. (2 sts)
Lift RH st over LH st. (1 st)
Pick up and k into cast-on edge by first
petal so that the daisy forms a circle.
Bind (cast) off.

Leaves
(make 4)
Using US 2/3 (3 mm) needles, cast on
2 sts in F.
Row 1: [Inc1] twice. (4 sts)
Row 2: P.
Row 3: [Inc1, k1] twice. (6 sts)
Work 7 rows in st st beg with a p row.
Row 11: Ssk, k2, k2tog. (4 sts)
Row 12: P.
Row 13: Ssk, k2tog. (2 sts)
Row 14: P.
Row 15: K2tog. (1 st)
Break yarn and pull rem st through.

Making up and finishing
• Place the Cozy over the teapot so that
the center split short edges are at the
front, near the spout. Join the seam
using mattress stitch (see page 23),
leaving a gap for the spout. Join the top
part and lower edge of the seam on the
handle side of the pot using mattress
stitch. Sew the two ends of the crochet

chain Loop to the top of the cozy.
• Join the main seam of each Bee using
mattress stitch, stuffing the bee lightly
as you go. Gather each pair of Wings
across the center and fasten to the
back of a Bee, using the photograph
(opposite) as a guide.
• Sew the Bees, Daisies, and Leaves in
place. Using cream thread, sew buttons
to Daisy centers.

Lampshade Cover

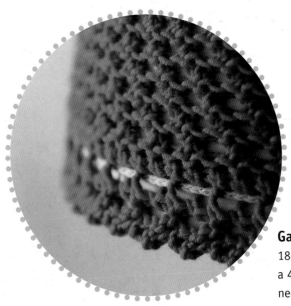

Add a touch of vintage chic to a boring old lampshade with this gorgeous cover. We have knitted it in a dramatic shade of red—but you might fancy something pale and equally groovy. The cover features two types of easy lace knit and a special binding (casting) off stitch that creates a picot edge. So it's not for complete beginners—but if you're up for a bit of a challenge, we guarantee you'll love the results.

Yarn and other materials

Sublime Baby Cashmere Merino Silk DK
(75% extra fine merino wool, 20% silk, 5% cashmere) light worsted (DK) yarn
• 3 x 1¾ oz/50 g balls (378 yd/348 m) in shade 192 Teddy Red (A)
Rowan Cashsoft DK (57% extra fine merino, 33% microfiber, 10% cashmere) light worsted (DK) yarn
• Small amount of 509 Lime (B)

• Drum-style lampshade in pale beige, measuring 7½ in. (19 cm) tall x 9 in. (23 cm) diameter at top

Needles and equipment

• Size US 5 (3.75 mm) and size US 6 (4 mm) knitting needles
• Size US G6 (4 mm) crochet hook
• Yarn sewing needle
• Small safety pin to thread the cord

Gauge (tension)

18 sts and 22 rows over main pattern to a 4-in. (10-cm) square on US 6 (4 mm) needles.

Measurements

The cover will fit a standard lampshade measuring 7½ in. (19 cm) high and 9 in. (23 cm) top diameter.

Abbreviations

See page 11.

Cover

LOWER EDGE
(make 1)
Using US 5 (3.75 mm) needles, cast on 7 sts in A.
Row 1: K1, [k2tog, yo twice] twice, k2. (9 sts)
Row 2: K3, [p1, k2] twice.
Row 3: K1, k2tog, yo twice, k2tog, k4.
Row 4: Bind (cast) off 2 sts (1 st rem on RH needle), k3, p1, k2. (7 sts)
Rep last 4 rows 47 times more.
Bind (cast) off.

MAIN SECTION
(make 1)
Using US 6 (4 mm) needles and A, pick up and k 98 sts across straight edge of top edging.
K 2 rows
Row 3: P1, [yrn, p2tog] to last st, p1.
K 3 rows.
Rep last 4 rows 17 times more.
Row 75: Cast on 2 sts, bind (cast) off 4 sts [sl st rem on RH needle back to LH needle, cast on 2 sts, bind (cast) off 4 sts] to end.

Cord

Using crochet hook, work a 39-in. (1-m) crochet chain in B.

Making up and finishing

• Join side seam of Cover using flat stitch (see page 23).
• Weave yarn tails at each end of the Cord back into itself. Using a small safety pin, thread the Cord in and out of the lower edge, using the photograph (above) as a guide.
• Place the Cover over the lampshade and tie the Cord in a bow.

Dog Draft Excluder

When there's a wind blowing outside, there's nothing better than a low-tech draft excluder to keep the breeze at bay. This knitted sausage dog will help keep you warm and cozy—and add a quirky touch to your interior. He's knitted in a lovely soft gray yarn and we've given him a rich purple coat so that you can be sure that he will keep warm too!

Yarn and other materials

Debbie Bliss Rialto Aran (100% extra fine merino wool) worsted (Aran) yarn
• 4 x 1¾ oz/50 g balls (352 yd/320 m) of 29 Mid Grey (A)
Sirdar Country Style DK (40% nylon, 30% wool, 30% acrylic) light worsted (DK) yarn
• 1 x 1¾ oz/50 g ball (170 yd/155 m) of 604 Damson (B)
Sublime Baby Cashmere Merino Silk DK (75% extra fine merino wool, 20% silk, 5% cashmere) light worsted (DK) yarn
• Small amount of 124 Splash (C)

• Very small amount of black light worsted (DK) yarn (D)
• 5¼ oz (150 g) fiberfill toy filling
• 2 x ½ in. (1 cm) black buttons
• ½ in. (1 cm) purple button for the collar
• Standard black and cream sewing thread

Needles and equipment

• Size US 5 (3.75 mm) and size US 3 (3.25 mm) knitting needles
• Stitch holder
• Yarn sewing needle
• Standard sewing needle

Gauge (tension)

18 sts and 24 rows in stockinette (stocking) stitch to a 4-in. (10-cm) square on US 5 (3.75 mm) needles.

Measurements

The dog measures 35 in. (89 cm) from tail to tip of nose and is suitable for a 30 in. (76 cm) wide internal door. The length can be altered easily by knitting more or fewer rows for the dog's body.

Abbreviations

See page 11.

Main body

(make 1)
Using US 5 (3.75 mm) needles, cast on 50 sts in A.
Work 192 rows in st st beg with a K row.
Row 193: K25, turn work, cast on 14 sts, leave rem 25 sts on stitch holder, and work on 39 sts just worked only.
Work 5 rows in st st beg with a p row.
Row 199: K2, k2tog, k to end. (38 sts)
Row 200: P.
Rep last 2 rows 6 times more. (32 sts)
Row 213: K2, k2tog, k to end. (31 sts)
Row 214: P to last 2 sts, p2tog. (30 sts)
Rep last 2 rows once more. (28 sts)
Row 217: Bind (cast) off 5 sts, k to end. (23 sts)
Row 218: P.
Row 219: K2, k2tog, k to end. (22 sts)
Row 220: P.
Rep last 2 rows 7 times more. (15 sts)
Row 235: K2, k2tog, k to end. (14 sts)
Row 236: P to last 2 sts, p2tog. (13 sts)
Rep last 2 rows 4 times more. (5 sts)
Bind (cast) off.
Rejoin yarn to sts on stitch holder.
Row 1: Cast on 14 sts, k to end. (39 sts)
Work 5 rows in st st beg with a p row.
Row 7: K to last 4 sts, ssk, k2. (38 sts)
Row 8: P.
Rep last 2 rows 6 times more. (32 sts)
Row 21: K to last 4 sts, ssk, k2. (31 sts)
Row 22: P2tog, p to end. (30 sts)
Rep last 2 rows once more. (28 sts)

Row 25: K.
Row 26: Bind (cast) off 5 sts pwise, p to end. (23 sts)
Row 27: K to last 4 sts, ssk, k2. (22 sts)
Row 28: P.
Rep last 2 rows 7 times more. (15 sts)
Row 43: K to last 4 sts, ssk, k2. (14 sts)
Row 44: P2tog, p to end. (13 sts)
Rep last 2 rows 4 times more. (5 sts)
Bind (cast) off.

Ears
(make 4 pieces)
Using US 5 (3.75 mm) needles, cast on 6 sts in A.
Row 1: Inc1, k to last 2 sts, inc1, k1. (8 sts)
Row 2: P.

Row 3: K1, M1, k to last st, M1, k1.
(10 sts)
Row 4: P.
Rep last 2 rows twice more. (14 sts)
Work 18 rows in st st beg with a k row.
Row 27: K2, k2tog, k to last 4 sts, ssk,
k2. (12 sts)
Work 7 rows in st st beg with a p row.
Bind (cast) off.

Tail

(make 1)
Using US 5 (3.75 mm) needles, cast on
14 sts in A.
Work 14 rows in st st beg with a k row.
Row 15: K1, k2tog, k to last 3 sts, ssk,
k1. (12 sts)
Work 5 rows in st st beg with a p row.
Row 21: K1, k2tog, k to last 3 sts, ssk,
k1. (10 sts)
Work 3 rows in st st beg with a p row.
Rep last 4 rows once more. (8 sts)
Row 29: K1, k2tog, k2, ssk, k1. (6 sts)
Row 30: P2tog, p2, p2tog. (4 sts)
Bind (cast) off.

Coat

(make 1)
Using US 3 (3.25 mm) needles, cast on
20 sts in B.
Row 1: Inc1, k to last 2 sts, inc1, k1.
(22 sts)
Rep last row twice more. (26 sts)
Row 4: K3, p to last 3 sts, k3.
Row 5: K.
Row 6: K3, p to last 3 sts, k3.
Rep last 2 rows 47 times more.
Row 101: K1, ssk, k to last 3 sts, k2tog,
k1. (24 sts)
Row 102: K3, p to last 3 sts, k3.

Rep last 2 rows once more. (22 sts)
Bind (cast) off.

Coat strap

(make 1)
Using US 3 (3.25 mm) needles, cast on
18 sts in B.
Row 1: K.
Row 2: K3, p to last 3 sts, k3.
Rep last 2 rows 21 times more.
Bind (cast) off.

Collar

(make 1)
Using US 3 (3.25 mm) needles, cast on
6 sts in C.
Row 1: K.
Row 2: K1, p to last st, k1.
Rep last 2 rows 36 times more.
Row 75: K2, bind (cast) off 2 sts, k to
end. (4 sts)
Row 76: K1, p1, turn work and cast on
2 sts, turn work again, p1, k1. (6 sts)
K 2 rows.
Bind (cast) off.

Making up and finishing

• Sew the top head, back, and underside
seams of the Main body using mattress
stitch (see page 23) and leaving a 6-in.
(15-cm) gap in the underside for filling.
Stuff the dog and close the gap.
• Place two Ear pieces RS together and
oversew round the curved edges, then
turn the ear RS out. Repeat for the other
ear. Oversew the Ears in place.
• Join the long edges of the Tail using
mattress stitch. Stuff very lightly and
oversew in place using the photograph
as a guide.

• Sew two button eyes in place with
black thread and work a small coil of
Chain Stitch (see page 24) using D for
the nose. Work a Straight Stitch (see
page 24) using D for the mouth.
• Oversew the Coat in place. Position the
Strap around the dog and oversew the
short ends to the Coat.
• Sew the button on the Collar with
cream thread and place the Collar round
the dog's neck.

Market Bag

This roomy bag is just the thing to take on a big shopping trip. It is knitted in an easy lace pattern that makes it light to carry and nice and stretchy. The machine-washable yarn, which contains both cotton and wool, is soft and smooth—and mega chunky, so it knits up really quickly. We've added a perky flower to give our bag that extra pizzazz—but you could leave it plain if you prefer.

Yarn and other materials

Sirdar Denim Ultra (60% acrylic, 25% cotton, 15% wool) chunky yarn
• 3 x 3½ oz/100 g balls (246 yd/225 m) of 655 Bakery (A)

Patons Diploma Gold DK (55% wool, 25% acrylic, 20% nylon) light worsted (DK) yarn
• 1 x 1¾ oz/50 g ball (131 yd/120 m) of 6243 Bright Aqua (B)

Sublime Baby Cashmere Merino Silk DK (75% extra fine merino wool, 20% silk, 5% cashmere) light worsted (DK) yarn
• Very small amount of 192 Teddy Red (C)

• Standard cream sewing thread
• ½ in. (1 cm) pale pink button

Needles and equipment
• Size US 15 (10 mm) and size US 6 (4 mm) knitting needles
• Size US 7 (4.5 mm) crochet hook
• Yarn sewing needle
• Standard sewing needle

Gauge (tension)
10 sts and 14 rows in A over main pattern to a 4-in. (10-cm) square on US 15 (10 mm) needles.

Measurements
The bag is approx. 15 x 16 in. (38 x 40 cm), excluding strap.

Abbreviations
See page 11.

Main bag
(make 2 pieces)
Using US 15 (10 mm) needles, cast on 34 sts in A.
Row 1: Inc1, k to last 2 sts, inc1, k1. (36 sts)
Row 2: K.
Row 3: Inc1, k to last 2 sts, inc1, k1. (38 sts)
Row 4: P1, [yrn, p2tog] to last st, p1. K 3 rows.
Row 8: P1, [p2tog, yrn] to last st, p1. K 3 rows.
Row 12: P1, [yrn, p2tog] to last st, p1. K 3 rows.

Row 16: P1, [p2tog, yrn] to last st, p1. K 3 rows.
Rep last 8 rows 4 times more.
Row 52: P1, [yrn, p2tog] to last st, p1. K 3 rows.
Row 56: P1, [p2tog, yrn] to last st, p1.
Row 57: K.
Bind (cast) off.

Strap
(make 1)
Using US 15 (10 mm) needles, cast on 6 sts in A.

K 132 rows.
Bind (cast) off.

Flower

PETALS

(make 1 piece)

Using US 6 (4 mm) needles, cast on 15 sts in B, using yarn double.

Row 1: [Inc1] twice, k1.

*Turn and work on 5 sts just knitted only.

Row 2: K1, p3, k1.

Row 3: Inc1, k to last 2 sts, inc1, k1. (7 sts)

Row 4: K1, p to last st, k1.

Row 5: K.

Row 6: K1, p to last st, k1.

Rep last 2 rows 10 times more.

Row 27: K1, ssk, k1, k2tog, k1. (5 sts)

Row 28: P2tog, p1, p2tog. (3 sts)

Row 29: Bind (cast) off 2 sts (1 st rem on RH needle), [pick up and k 1 st, bind (cast) off 1 st] 9 times down side of petal.

Row 30: (1 st rem on RH needle), k1 (from original cast-on sts on LH needle), inc1, k1.**

Rep from * to ** 3 times.

Turn and work on 5 sts just knitted only.

Next row: K1, p3, k1.

Next row: Inc1, k to last 2 sts, inc1, k1. (7 sts)

Next row: K1, p to last st, k1.

Next row: K.

Next row: K1, p to last st, k1.

Rep last 2 rows 10 times more.

Next row: K1, ssk, k1, k2tog, k1. (5 sts)

Next row: P2tog, p1, p2tog. (3 sts)

Next row: Bind (cast) off 2 sts (1 st rem on RH needle), [pick up and k 1 st, bind (cast) off 1 st] 9 times down side of petal.

Break yarn and pull through rem st.

CENTER

(make 1)

Using US 6 (4 mm) needles, cast on 14 sts in C, using yarn double.

Row 1: K.

Row 2: [Cast on 2 sts, bind (cast) off 4 sts, sl st rem on RH needle to LH needle] to end.

Fasten off.

Making up and finishing

• Join the side and lower seams of the Main Bag using mattress stitch (see page 23). Oversew the Handle ends in place. Using three strands of B and the crochet hook, work a crochet edging (see page 25) round the Handle sides and top of the Main Bag, using the photograph (left) as a guide.

• Join the two edges of the base of the Petals to form a circle. Join the two short edges of the flower Center to form a circle. Stitch the Center in the middle of the Petal piece and stitch the flower in place using the photograph (above) as a guide. Using cream thread, sew a button in position onto the flower center.

Wallet

If you're fed up with all those boring wallets out there, why not give your money and bank cards a treat and knit them their own cozy home? This cute case is knitted in a firm textured stitch in a smooth, soft yarn. It has two pockets for cards and a separate pocket for bank notes. We've brightened our wallet up with a bright pink button but, of course, the color choices are up to you.

Yarn and other materials

Rowan Cashsoft DK (57% extra fine merino, 33% microfiber, 10% cashmere) light worsted (DK) yarn
• 1 x 1¾ oz/50 g ball (125 yd/115 m) of shade 509 Lime (A)

Sirdar Country Style DK (40% nylon, 30% wool, 30% acrylic) light worsted (DK) yarn
• 1 x 1¾ oz/50 g ball (170 yd/155 m) of shade 409 Naturelle (B)

• ¾ in. (2 cm) bright pink button
• ⅝ in. (1.5 cm) snap fastener
Standard cream sewing thread

Needles and equipment
• Size US 2/3 (3 mm) knitting needles
• Yarn sewing needle
• Standard sewing needle

Gauge (tension)

25 sts and 28 rows over main pattern on outer part of wallet to a 4-in. (10-cm) square on US 2/3 (3 mm) needles.

Measurements

The wallet measures 4 x 5½ in. (10 x 14 cm) when closed.

Abbreviations

See page 11.

Main wallet

(make 1)

Cast on 35 sts in A.

K 2 rows.

Row 3: K2, p to last 2 sts, k2.

Row 4: K5, p1, [k5, p1] to last 5 sts, k5.

Row 5: K2, p2, k1, p1, k1, [p3, k1, p1, k1] to last 4 sts, p2, k2.

Row 6: K3, p1, [k3, p1, k1, p1] to last 7 sts, k3, p1, k3.

Row 7: K3, [p5, k1] to last 2 sts, k2.

Row 8: K3, p1, [k3, p1, k1, p1] to last 7 sts, k3, p1, k3.

Row 9: K2, p2, k1, p1, k1, [p3, k1, p1, k1] to last 4 sts, p2, k2.

Rep last 6 rows 5 times more.

Row 40: K5, p1, [k5, p1] to last 5 sts, k5.

K 5 rows.

Row 46: K5, p1, [k5, p1] to last 5 sts, k5.

Row 47: K2, p2, k1, p1, k1, [p3, k1, p1, k1] to last 4 sts, p2, k2.

Row 48: K3, p1, [k3, p1, k1, p1] to last 7 sts, k3, p1, k3.

Row 49: K3, [p5, k1] to last 2 sts, k2.

Row 50: K3, p1, [k3, p1, k1, p1] to last 7 sts, k3, p1, k3.

Row 51: K2, p2, k1, p1, k1, [p3, k1, p1, k1] to last 4 sts, p2, k2.

Rep last 6 rows 5 times more.

Row 82: K5, p1, [k5, p1] to last 5 sts, k5.

K 2 rows.

Bind (cast) off.

Lining

(make 1)

The inner is knitted from the card pocket edge to the note pocket edge.

Cast on 34 sts in B.

K2 rows.

Work 17 rows in st st beg with a k row.

Now begin with a k row to work the RS of st st on the other side.

Work 31 rows in st st beg with a k row.

K 5 rows.

Work 35 rows in st st beg with a k row.

Now begin with a k row to work the RS of st st on the other side.

Work 23 rows in st st beg with a k row.

K 2 rows.

Bind (cast) off.

Closure

(make 1)

Cast on 12 sts in A.

Row 1: K.

Row 2: K2, p to last 2 sts, k2.

Rep last 2 rows 7 times more.

Row 17: K.

Row 18: K2tog, k to last 2 sts, ssk.

Bind (cast) off 10 sts.

Making up and finishing

• Fold the two sides of the Lining toward the center to form the two pocket sections and oversew at the sides, very close to the edge. Work a line of Chain Stitch (see page 24) along the center of the card pocket to form two equal sections.

• Oversew the Lining to the Main Wallet, making sure the central garter stitch columns line up. The Lining should be sewn just inside the outer edge of the Main Wallet.

• Oversew the Closure in position on the underside of the wallet. Sew one half of the snap fastener on the underside of the Closure and the other half to match to it on the top face of the wallet. Sew the button on the outside of the Closure.

Yarn and other materials

SMC Select Extra Soft Merino (100% merino wool) light worsted (DK) yarn
• 2 x 1¾ oz/50 g balls (284 yd/260 m) in each of 5106 Purple (A), 5148 Violet (C), and 5105 Lilac (E)

Sublime Extra Fine Merino Wool DK (100% merino wool) light worsted (DK) yarn
• 4 x 1¾ oz/50 g balls (508 yd/464 m) of 003 Alabaster (B)

Sublime Baby Cashmere Merino Silk DK (75% extra fine merino wool, 20% silk, 5% cashmere) light worsted (DK) yarn
• 2 x 1¾ oz/50 g balls (252 yd/232 m) of 001 Piglet (D)

Needles and equipment
• US 9 (5.5 mm) circular knitting needle
• Yarn sewing needle

Gauge (tension)
20 sts and 20 rows in main pattern to a 4-in. (10-cm) square on US 9 (5.5 mm) needle.

Stripy Throw

This wavy striped throw is knitted in assorted soft yarns in a delightfully simple lace stitch that is strangely addictive. It can be draped over the back of a chair, stretched across the end of a bed, or pulled over your knees to keep out the winter chill. We've knitted it in an assortment of cream, pinks, and mauves—but you can, of course, knit it in any shades you want to complement your own color scheme.

Measurements
The throw measures approx. 25 x 51 in. (64 x 130 cm).

Throw
(make 1)
Cast on 128 sts in A.
Row 1 (RS): K.
Row 2: P.
Row 3: K1, *[k2tog] 3 times, [yo, k1] 6 times, [k2tog] 3 times; rep from * to last st, k1.
Row 4: K.
Rep these 4 rows 4 times more.
Break A and join in B.
Row 21: K.
Row 22: P.
Row 23: K1, *[k2tog] 3 times, [yo, k1] 6 times, [k2tog] 3 times; rep from * to last st, k1.
Row 24: K.
Rep these 4 rows 4 times more.
Break B and join C.
Row 41: K.
Row 42: P.
Row 43: K1, *[k2tog] 3 times, [yo, k1] 6 times, [k2tog] 3 times; rep from * to last st, k1.

Row 44: K.
Rep these 4 rows 4 times more.
Break C and join B.
Row 61: K.
Row 62: P.
Row 63: K1, *[k2tog] 3 times, [yo, k1] 6 times, [k2tog] 3 times; rep from * to last st, k1.
Row 64: K.
Rep these 4 rows 4 times more.
Break B and join D.
Row 81: K.
Row 82: P.
Row 83: K1, *[k2tog] 3 times, [yo, k1] 6 times, [k2tog] 3 times; rep from * to last st, k1.
Row 84: K.
Rep these 4 rows 4 times more.
Break D and join B.
Row 101: K.
Row 102: P.
Row 103: K1, *[k2tog] 3 times, [yo, k1] 6 times, [k2tog] 3 times; rep from * to last st, k1.
Row 104: K.
Rep these 4 rows 4 times more.
Break B and join E.
Row 121: K.

Row 122: P.

Row 123: K1, *[k2tog] 3 times, [yo, k1] 6 times, [k2tog] 3 times; rep from * to last st, k1.

Row 124: K.

Rep these 4 rows 4 times more.

Break E and join B.

Row 141: K.

Row 142: P.

Row 143: K1, *[k2tog] 3 times, [yo, k1] 6 times, [k2tog] 3 times; rep from * to last st, k1.

Row 144: K.

Rep these 4 rows 4 times more.

Break B and join D.

Row 161: K.

Row 162: P.

Row 163: K1, *[k2tog] 3 times, [yo, k1] 6 times, [k2tog] 3 times; rep from * to last st, k1.

Row 164: K.

Rep these 4 rows 4 times more.

Break D and join B.

Row 181: K.

Row 182: P.

Row 183: K1, *[k2tog] 3 times, [yo, k1] 6 times, [k2tog] 3 times; rep from * to last st, k1.

Row 184: K.

Rep these 4 rows 4 times more.

Break B and join C.

Row 201: K.

Row 202: P.

Row 203: K1, *[k2tog] 3 times, [yo, k1] 6 times, [k2tog] 3 times; rep from * to last st, k1.

Row 204: K.

Rep these 4 rows 4 times more.

Break C and join B.

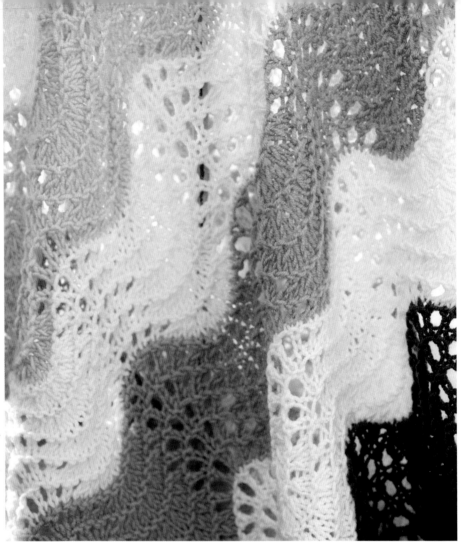

Row 221: K.

Row 222: P.

Row 223: K1, *[k2tog] 3 times, [yo, k1] 6 times, [k2tog] 3 times; rep from * to last st, k1.

Row 224: K.

Rep these 4 rows 4 times more.

Break B and join A.

Row 241: K.

Row 242: P.

Row 243: K1, *[k2tog] 3 times, [yo, k1] 6 times, [k2tog] 3 times; rep from * to last st, k1.

Row 244: K

Rep these 4 rows 4 times more.

K 1 row.

Bind (cast) off loosely.

Making up and finishing

• Sew in yarn ends.

Backpack

If you're looking for a handy home for those daily essentials, this cozy backpack is the perfect solution. Big enough to hold what you need and compact enough not to get in the way, it's knitted in a chunky yarn in a deep shade of teal—with accents in green and cream. The textured knit gives it shape and substance and is very easy to master. It is designed to fit an average adult but you can easily make it for a child or larger adult by knitting shorter or longer straps.

Yarn and other materials
Katia Peru (40% wool, 40% acrylic, 20% alpaca) chunky yarn
- 2 x 3½ oz/100 g balls (232 yd/212 m) of 34 Teal (A)
- 1 x 3½ oz/100 g ball (116 yd/106 m) each of 15 Green (B) and 07 Cream (C)
- 1¼ in. (3 cm) mother-of-pearl button
- Standard cream sewing thread

Needles and equipment
- Size US 10 (6 mm) knitting needles
- Yarn sewing needle
- Size US 7 (4.5 mm) crochet hook
- Small safety pin
- Standard sewing needle

Gauge (tension)

15 sts and 22 rows over main pattern to a 4-in. (10-cm) square on US 10 (6 mm) needles.

Measurements

The backpack is approx. 12 in. (30 cm) high and measures 11 in. (28 cm) across. The straps are 25 in. (64 cm) long, to fit an average size woman. They can be made shorter or longer by casting on fewer or more stitches.

Abbreviations

See page 11.

Front/Back

(make 2 the same)

Cast on 43 sts in A.

Row 1 (RS): K3, [s1 pwise, k3] to end.

Row 2: K3, [yfwd, s1 pwise, yb, k3] to end.

Row 3: K1, [s1 pwise, k3] to last 2 sts, s1 pwise, k1.

Row 4: P1, s1 pwise, [p3, s1 pwise] to last st, p1.

Rep last 4 rows 16 times more.

Break A and join in B.

K 2 rows.

Row 71: K3, [yo, k2tog, k2] to end.

K 2 rows.

Bind (cast) off.

Top flap

(make 1)

Cast on 25 sts in A.

Row 1 (RS): K6, [s1 pwise, k3] to last 3 sts, k3.

Row 2: K6, [yfwd, s1 pwise, yb, k3] to last 3 sts, k3.

Row 3: K4, [s1 pwise, k3] to last 5 sts, s1 pwise, k4.

Row 4: K3, p1, s1 pwise, [p3, s1 pwise] to last 4 sts, p1, k3.

Rep last 4 rows 8 times more.

Row 37: K2, k2tog, k to last 4 sts, ssk, k2. (23 sts)

Rep last row twice more. (19 sts)

Row 40: K8, bind (cast) off 3 sts, k to end. (16 sts)

Row 41: K8, cast on 3 sts, k to end. (19 sts)

Bind (cast) off.

Straps

(make 2)

Cast on 94 sts in B.

K 6 rows.

Bind (cast) off.

Cord

(make 1)

Using the crochet hook, make a 39-in. (1-m) chain in C.

Pompoms

(make 2)

Wrap C round four fingers of one hand about 26 times. Remove and tie a separate length of C very tightly round the middle, taking one yarn end in and out of the center of the yarn bundle several times to make it very secure. Trim and shape the looped ends of the bundle to form a pompom about 1½ in. (3.5–4 cm) in diameter.

Making up and finishing

• Join the Front and Back along sides and lower edge using mattress stitch (see page 23). Oversew the Top flap in place on the center back of the bag, just below the eyelet border.

• Secure one end of the Cord to one of the Pompoms. Using the safety pin, thread the other end through the eyelets at the top of the backpack, starting at the center. Secure the second pompom in place on the other end of the Cord.

• Oversew the short edges of the Straps in place at the two lower corners of the bag and to either side of the center top, just below the eyelet border. Using cream thread, sew the button in place.

Suppliers

US

Knitting Fever Inc.
PO Box 336
315 Bayview Avenue
Amityville
NY 11701
Tel: +1 516 546 3600
www.knittingfever.com
Debbie Bliss, Katia, Sirdar, Sublime

Westminster Fibers
165 Ledge Street
Nashua
NH 03060
Tel: +800 445 9276
www.westmnsterfibers.com
Rowan

CANADA

Diamond Yarn
155 Martin Ross Unit 3
Toronto, ON
M3J 2L9
Tel: +1 416 736 6111
www.diamondyarn.com
Debbie Bliss, Katia, Sirdar, Sublime

Patons
320 Livingstone Avenue South
Box 40
Listowel, ON
N4W 3H3
Tel: +1 888 368 8401
www.patonsyarns.com

Westminster Fibers
10 Roybridge Gate Suite 200
Vaughn, ON
L4H 3MB
Tel: +800 445 9276
www.westmnsterfibers.com
Rowan

UK

Debbie Bliss Yarns
Designer Yarns Ltd
Units 8–10 Newbridge Industrial Estate
Pitt Street, Keighly
West Yorkshire BD21 4PQ
Tel: +44 (0) 1535 664222
www.debbieblissonline.com

Katia Yarns
Barcelona, Spain
Tel: +34 93 828 38 19
www.katia.com
Website gives details of local
UK suppliers

King Cole
King Cole Ltd
Merrie Mills
Elliot Street, Silsden
West Yorkshire BD20 0DE
Tel: +44 (0) 1535 650230
www.kingcole.co.uk

Patons
Coats Crafts UK
Green Lane Mill
Holmfirth
West Yorkshire HD9 2DX
Tel +44 (0) 1484 681881
www.coatscrafts.co.uk

Rowan
Rowan Yarns
Green Lane Mill
Holmfirth
West Yorkshire HD9 2DX
Tel: +44 (0) 1484 681881
www.knitrowan.com

Sirdar
Sirdar Spinning Ltd
Flanshaw Lane
Wakefield
West Yorkshire WF2 9ND
Tel: +44 (0) 1924 231682
www.sirdar.co.uk

Deramores
Online store only
Tel: 0845 519 457

www.deramores.com
Patons, Sublime, Twilleys, Wendy

Mavis Crafts
Online and retail store
Tel: +44 (0) 208 950 5445
www.mavis-crafts.com
Katia, Sirdar, Sublime, Wendy

John Lewis
Retail stores and online
www.johnlewis.com
Telephone numbers of local
stores on website
Tel: 08456 049 049

AUSTRALIA

Prestige Yarns Pty Ltd
PO Box 39
Bulli
NSW 2516
Tel: +61 (0)2 4285 6669
www.prestigeyarns.com
Debbie Bliss

Texyarns International PTY Ltd
105–115 Dover Street
Cremorne, Melbourne
VIC 3121
Tel: +61 (0)3 9427 9009
www.texyarns.com
Katia

Yarn Over
Shop 1 265 Baker Street
Keperra,
QLD 4054
Tel: +61 (0)7 3851 2608
Patons

Rowan
www.knitrowan.com
Online store locator

Creative Images
PO Box 106
Hastings
VIC 3915
Tel: +61 (0)3 5979 1555
Sirdar

Index

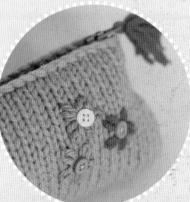

Acknowledgments

I would like to thank Cindy Richards and her team at Cico for coming up with the idea for this book, for asking me to get involved, and for their guidance. I would especially like to thank Marie Clayton, my pattern editor, and Marilyn Wilson, my very patient pattern checker. I would also like to thank Mick and Pam Conquest from Mavis's, my local yarn store in Hertfordshire, England.

Last but definitely not least, I'd like to thank my parents, Paddy and David Goble, for all their encouragement and support, and my partner Roger Dromard and son Louis for putting up with a house that sometimes looks more like a yarn store.